The Analyzed Bible

The
Analyzed Bible

Isaiah

Volume 2

G. Campbell
Morgan

BAKER BOOK HOUSE

Grand Rapids, Michigan 49506

First published 1910 by
Fleming H. Revell Company
Paperback edition issued 1984 by
Baker Book House

ISBN: 0-8010-6172-5

Printed in the United States of America

CONTENTS

PROPHECIES OF PEACE

Contents

Contents

Contents

PREFACE

ISAIAH was a prophet of Judah. He exercised his ministry wholly within her borders, and with a view to her correction and comfort. His burdens of the nations were uttered concerning those which surrounded Judah and had harassed her. His outlook was world-wide, and inclusive of the whole purpose of God. Profoundly conscious of the intention of God that through His people all peoples should be blessed, he saw through all the processes of judgment the ultimate blessing of the whole earth.

The book as a whole sets forth the two facts of Judgment and Peace, and shows their inter-relation in the economy of God. Dealing first with Judgment, his messages show how it ever proceeds to Peace. Dealing finally with Peace, they show how it is always conditioned in Righteousness. Between these principal parts of the book is an historical section, the first part of which is related to the Judgment prophecies, and the second to those concerning Peace.

Isaiah's messages were delivered during a dark period in the history of the people. He lived and taught during the reigns of Uzziah, Jotham, Ahaz, and Hezekiah. Contemporary with him, Hosea was prophesying to Israel, and Micah to Judah.

The unity of the teaching is conspicuous, and is the chief argument in favour of the unity of authorship.

The book naturally falls into three parts: Prophecies of Judgment (i.–xxxv.); Historical Interlude (xxxvi.–xxxix.); Prophecies of Peace (xl.–lxvii.).

Isaiah 2

ISAIAH

C. PROPHECIES OF PEACE

We now commence the study of the Prophecies of Peace which, like the Prophecies of Judgment, fall into three sections, dealing in turn with the purpose of peace; the Prince of peace; and the programme of peace.

I. THE PURPOSE OF PEACE

In declaring the purpose of peace the prophet first uttered a foreword of explanation; and then dealt successively with the majesty of Jehovah; the manifesto of Jehovah; the messages of Jehovah; the might of Jehovah; and the mercy of Jehovah.

Prologue

The first paragraph constitutes a prologue to the whole division. This prologue opens with a declaration which indicates the burden of all that is to follow; describes the making of a highway for God; and closes with a com-

mission to announce the good tidings to Jerusalem.

a. THE BURDEN

The opening words of this section, " Comfort
ye, comfort ye My people," reveal the burden of
all that is to follow to the end of the book. As
in the first division all the messages were based
upon the fact that the judgment of God proceeds to peace, so in this third, the master-
thought is that of the establishment of peace
by the processes of judgment. The supreme
note of the first division was that of judgment.
The supreme note of the last is that of peace.

It is important here that we should recognize the close connection of these opening
words with the closing paragraph of the first
division. As we have seen, the second division
is historic, and is only of value as the events
chronicled help to explain the reason and
method of the prophetic teaching. In the
prophecies of judgment the final outlook was
upon world-wide desolation, followed by world-
wide restoration. The last words of that section were, " Everlasting joy shall be upon their
heads: they shall obtain gladness and joy, and
sorrow and sighing shall flee away." The first
words of the present division are, " Comfort

ye, comfort ye My people, saith your God."
The connection and relation is self-evident.

The message of comfort to be delivered is
first summarized. The prophet is charged to
" speak comfortably," that is to the heart of
Jerusalem, because " her warfare," that is the
long-continued period of her trouble, " is accomplished," " her iniquity is pardoned," and
the measure of her chastisement is ended, seeing that she has received " double for all her
sins."

In all the earlier messages the dominant
thought was that the purpose of judgment is
peace. The burden of this last division is
that when judgment is accomplished, peace
will be the result.

b. THE HIGHWAY

In figurative language the prophet then described the way by which Jehovah would proceed to the accomplishment of this purpose.
Two voices were heard, the first telling of the
advent of Jehovah; and the second announcing
the certainty of His victory.

1. *The First Voice*

The first voice was one which called upon
the people to prepare the way of the Lord.

This involved the proclamation of His advent. There is a recognition of the desolation in the use of the words, " the wilderness " and " the desert "; and also of the restoration to be accomplished by the fact that the Lord is to pass through the wilderness, and find in the desert a highway for His progress.

A description of the preparation necessary then follows. The valleys of depression are to be lifted; and the obstructing mountains and hills are to be lowered; all is to be made straight and plain for the progress of Jehovah. Without entering into any details, the prophet then declared what the coming of Jehovah would mean. His glory would be revealed, and all flesh would see. The absolute certainty of these things lay in the fact that the mouth of the Lord had spoken it.

2. *The Second Voice*

The second voice bade the prophet, " Cry." With immediate readiness the response was an inquiry as to the nature of the proclamation, " What shall I cry? " The answer affirmed the frailty of humanity against the power of Jehovah as He moves forward upon the highway of His purpose. Again the certainty of His overcoming might is declared to be that "the word of our God shall stand for ever."

c. THE COMMISSION

The final movement in the Prologue is one which chronicles the fact of the commission given to the prophet, and of his obedience thereto. Two things were necessary to the declaration of the message. The first is that the messenger should ascend the high mountain, that is, that he should come to the place of vision. The second is that with strength, and without fear he should deliver his message.

The whole burden of the message was then given to him in the one brief and inclusive declaration, "Behold, your God." The eyes of the people had all too long been fixed, either upon their foes, or upon their own princes and rulers. The former had proved too strong for the latter. The latter had failed to fulfil their duties toward God and toward His people. Therefore the supreme and inclusive word of the prophecy of hope and comfort was, "Behold, your God."

The prophet immediately gave utterance to the twofold truth concerning Jehovah, which in subsequent messages he would explain in detail, both as to its nature and its method. The first declaration is concerning Jehovah as the mighty One, Who is coming for active administration, and Whose might is irresistible. The second is concerning Him in His Shepherd character. The first settles the question of the foes who will be unable to stand before Him. The second is prophetic of the restoration of the people who are scattered and wounded through the failure of their rulers.

i. THE MAJESTY OF JEHOVAH

In elaboration of his declaration of Jehovah
as the Mighty One, the prophet first presented
Him in His majesty. This he set forth as to
its essential nature; by comparison with false
gods; and as demonstrated in different ways.

a. ESSENTIAL

The essential majesty of Jehovah is revealed
first in His might. This is seen in the perfect
adjustment of creation; the measured waters,
heaven meted out, the dust comprehended,
mountains and hills weighed. Every phrase
suggests moreover, the perfect ease with which
Jehovah accomplishes these things. The
whole creation is seen as known, ordered, and
upheld by the might of Jehovah.

It is revealed also in the fact of His wisdom.
This is stated in the form of questions which
admit of no answer save such as recognize the
fact that Jehovah acts without instruction and
without advice.

This essential might is finally demonstrated
by His government of all that which, in un-
aided wisdom and all-sufficient might, He has
created. The things which man ever thinks
of as great—the nations, the isles of the sea,

the mountains, and the beasts—are characterized by their littleness when placed in comparison with Himself.

b. BY COMPARISON

In view of this manifestation of essential
might, the prophet then suggested, declined,
and proved the impossibility of, comparison.
The whole movement of the prophetic utterances was aimed at recalling the people from
their idolatry to the recognition, worship, and
service of Jehovah.   In successive deliverances
the comparison between idols and God will
be wrought out in fuller detail.   It is now
suggested in the form of questions.   In view
of the essential might, wisdom, and government of God as manifesting His majesty, the
inquiry is raised as to who can be likened to
Him; or what idea, apart from the truth concerning Himself, can be placed in comparison
with Him.   To the mind of the prophet the
question is enough to reveal the impossibility
of comparison.

He immediately turned however to the illustrations of idolatry, describing the image of
metal which the workman melts, and a gold-
smith covers with gold, and the image of wood
made of the most durable tree.   These are the

work of men who are desirous of gods that
will last.   The whole of their effort is demonstration of this desire; and yet as the prophet
describes their activity, their failure is self-
evident.   He does not argue the impossibility
of comparison, because it is unnecessary to do
so.   The vision of the majesty of Jehovah in
the might and wisdom of His creation, and in
the perfect ease of His government, reveals
the unutterable folly of any attempt to sup-
plant Him by the feeble work of men who themselves are as nothing when compared with
Jehovah.

c. DEMONSTRATED

Finally the prophet showed that the majesty
of Jehovah is demonstrated in creation; in
actual government on earth and in the
heavens; and in the method of grace with
Israel.

1. *Creation*

The people were reminded of the majesty
of Jehovah in creation by allusions to their
own sacred writings as the prophet inquired if
they had not known, or heard, or been told
the story of beginnings, and of the foundations

of the earth. To accept the truth of the declarations with which they were familiar must
be to recognize the superlative and incompa-
rable majesty of Jehovah.

2. *Government*

That majesty is seen moreover, in His perfect government. He sits enthroned above the
circle of the earth, and in His presence humanity is infinitely small. The whole created
order He encompasses as He stretches the
heavens around the earth as a curtain, and
constitutes them a tent in which He dwells
Himself. The figure is one of striking beauty
and suggestiveness. By it the prophet calls
attention to the earth and the encompassing
firmament, like a curtain of gauze, as the
Hebrew word suggests; and reminds them that
within that curtain, enwrapping the whole
earth, is the presence of Jehovah. That is not
His final and only dwelling-place. It is but
a tent, and suggests His nearness to all the
earth and the inhabitants thereof. This God
is more than a presence. He is actively reigning, and within that activity the great ones
of the earth are completely under His control,
and of themselves, as apart from His will,
find no stability.

That government moreover, extends to the heavens which like a curtain form His tent of nearness to the affairs of earth. Again challenging men as to whom they will liken God, he bids them gaze beyond the earth, and into the wonders of the heavens, and see that these also have their origin in God; that His government is over them; that by His wisdom they are marshalled as an army; and in His strength they are upheld and sustained.

3. *Grace*

Finally turning to the people in direct address, and appealing to them on the basis of their history, the prophet demonstrated the majesty of God as revealed in His grace. The darkness of the circumstances in the midst of which these words were spoken, and the failure of their vision, had led them to an unbelief which declared that their way was hid from Jehovah, and their judgment passed away from God. In the light of the truths which the prophet had been re-enforcing as to the nearness and government of God, he inquired as to why they should make such assertions.

Did they not know His inherent strength, that the everlasting One, the Creator, was incapable of fainting or of weariness?

This strength moreover, was at the disposal
of those in need of it. All human strength
in itself inevitably fails. Even the youths and
the young men, those in the period of life
characterized by buoyancy and ability, must
inevitably faint and fail and fall. Humanity
rightly related to God cannot so fail. The
condition of strength is that men should wait
upon the Lord. When that condition is fulfilled, even though there is a fainting and a
weariness, there is also a renewal of strength.
The experience of such renewal the prophet
described in words remarkably chosen and
arranged so as to reveal the greatness of the
strength available to those who wait upon the
Lord. Whereas we might be inclined to think
that the progress of ability would be from
walking to running, and from running to fly-
ing, the prophet commences with flight, and
then speaks of running, and finally of walking.
Herein he recognizes the true and deepest experience of human need. In the day when it
is possible to spread the wings and fly, there
is less consciousness of the need of help than
in the day of running upon the dusty highway; and the hour when man is most conscious
of the need of help is that in which he can no
longer spread his wings in flight, or hasten
along the highway, but must walk patiently

and persistently. Yet for all these days there is strength in God. In the day of flight, those who wait upon the Lord mount as eagles, that is, with perfect ease. In the day of running, those who wait upon Him are able to continue without weariness. In the day of walking, they are able to walk without fainting.

The majesty of Jehovah is revealed to men by the grace in which with patience He succours and sustains His failing and fainting people, even more than by the splendour of His government of the universe, or by the awe-inspiring wonder of His creative might and wisdom.

ii. THE MANIFESTO OF JEHOVAH

Having thus announced the majesty of Jehovah, the prophet proceeded to utter His manifesto. This manifesto falls into three parts. The first consists of an introductory challenge; the second contains the central proclamation; while in the third the prophet utters his resultant appeal.

a. THE INTRODUCTORY CHALLENGE

In this section there are four movements. In the first Jehovah challenges the people as to Cyrus; in the second He declares His purpose of peace for Israel; in the third He repeats His challenge, but this time to the idols; and in the fourth He answers His own challenge.

1. *The Challenge of Jehovah as to Cyrus*

Jehovah calls the islands and the people to come near to judgment, that is, to consider what He has to say.

He then challenges them as though they were living in the midst of the circumstances which he foretells.[1] The challenge opens and closes

---

[1] It may be as well for the writer immediately to draw the reader's attention to the fact that he treats these prophecies as predictions, rather than as meditations after the events.

The fact that Isaiah could know nothing naturally, or by

with the question "Who?" Between these in-
quiries, the campaign of Cyrus is described.
In reading the paragraph it is important that
we should observe the difference between the
pronouns when they refer to Cyrus, and when
they refer to Someone Who is acting behind
and through Cyrus. In the declaration, "He
giveth nations before him, and maketh him
rule over kings," both these persons appear;
the "He" having reference to Someone author-
izing and empowering Cyrus; the "him" having reference to Cyrus himself. That is also
true in the next declaration, "He giveth them
as dust to his sword, as the driven stubble
to his bow." The supreme Person is described

the foresight of a statesman, of the events he described, does
not for a moment matter. It rather adds value to the writing.

Of course those who commence by denying the possibility
of prediction must discover some other explanation of these
writings. Those, on the other hand, who believe with Peter
that men spake from God as they were *borne along* ("as a ship
is carried and caught along by a mighty wind," Rotherham)
into the distant scenes, have no such difficulty.

As Dr. Thirtle points out, that which impressed Cyrus,
according to the tradition handed down by Josephus, was the
"*venerable age*" of the document in which he found a "fore-
cast of the offices which he could discharge, and these asso-
ciated with his very name."

Of course again, if prediction is *per se* impossible, then
Josephus' tradition is discredited. But is prediction impossible by God through men? If not, then the discrediting
of a tradition upon an unproven hypothesis does not prove
the tradition to be untrue.

by the first pronoun " He "; and Cyrus as instrument by the pronoun " his." In the third
part of the declaration the singular pronouns
all refer to Cyrus. " He pursueth them and
passeth on safely; even by a way that he had
not gone with his feet." Thus Cyrus is seen
passing on his conquering way, and that way
is that of victory over new territory. The
challenge is as to Who is acting behind Cyrus,
and using him.

The answer is then given, " I the Lord, the
first, and with the last, I am He."

In the presence of the victorious campaign
of Cyrus the peoples will be filled with con-
sternation, and will resort to methods to en-
sure their safety. All this is described. The
fear of the peoples is first set forth, then the
confederacy by which they will encourage each
other is declared, and finally a picture is given
of the making of new gods, evidently with the
hope that they will deliver the people from
the conquering might of Cyrus. Thus in the
challenge there is a recognition of the comparison or contrast described by the prophet
when he was dealing with the majesty of
Jehovah. He is seen using Cyrus, while men
make gods to deliver them from Cyrus.

2. *The Purpose of Peace for Israel*

In immediate contrast with the picture of the troubled peoples, there follows a declaration of Jehovah's purpose of peace for His own people. They are chosen and kept. Looking back they are seen as the seed of Abraham, the friend of God. At the present moment in spite of all their troubles, they are not cast away; and the promise is made to them of Jehovah's abiding presence, and of His continued activity on their behalf.

This activity is then set forth in the declaration that all their enemies shall suffer discomfiture, and that Israel seeking for their foes shall be unable to find them. All this as the result of Jehovah's help.

Finally their restoration is promised, first to that strength which will enable them to overcome their enemies; secondly to that prosperity which is expressed under the figure of material well-being and fruitfulness; and finally to the fulfilment of the original purpose for which the nation was created, that namely of witness to other peoples and nations, of the power and government of Jehovah.

3. *The Challenge repeated*

Again the challenge of Jehovah is heard. In the previous case it was a challenge to the people as to who was God. This time it is a challenge to the false gods, and calls upon them to produce proofs of their intelligence and ability. They are asked first to explain the past; and then to foretell the future; or finally with evident satire, to do something either good or bad which may make an impression.

The challenge ends with a word of supreme contempt, which declares that they have no being, that they are able to do nothing; and consequently affirms the wickedness of those who worship them.

4. *Jehovah's Answer to His own Challenge*

The last movement in this introductory challenge is one in which Jehovah answers in detail the questions asked. In the first place, speaking of the future as present, He again definitely declares that it is He Who has raised up Cyrus, and Who has ordered his victorious campaign.

Having made this claim, the comparison between the false gods and Jehovah is again made by the repetition of an inquiry, as to who had declared these things beforehand, for whoever had done so must be vindicated by the fulfilment of prediction. Among the false gods there had been no speech. Jehovah had declared, and had given to Jerusalem "One that bringeth good tidings."

The conclusion of the introductory movement is that of the declaration of the silence of the gods, and consequently of the vanity of idolatry.

b. THE CENTRAL PROCLAMATION

The manifesto now presents the great Servant of Jehovah. In the introductory challenge Jehovah has revealed Himself as governing the affairs of men, as He has claimed that even Cyrus the conqueror acts under His control; and as He has revealed His ideal of persistent purpose for Israel as His chosen servant. The prophetic vision now sees that government focussed in a Person Who acts, not merely as Cyrus does, under the compulsion of Jehovah, but in conscious harmony with Him; and Who unlike Israel, who has failed and necessitated the action of the Divine patience, never fails, but abides the perfect instrument of the Divine government, both in grace and in judgment.

This central proclamation falls into two parts. The first focusses attention upon the Servant of Jehovah; while the second presents Jehovah in His relationship to His Servant.

1. *The Servant of Jehovah*

The proclamation of the prophet first deals with the manifestation of One Who fulfils the perfect ideal of the Servant. In Himself He is described by Jehovah as " My Servant," and is seen as One upheld by Jehovah.

In His personal relation to Jehovah He is described by Jehovah as " My Chosen," and as One in Whom Jehovah delights.

His equipment for service is described by Jehovah as " My Spirit," and that Spirit is put upon Him by Jehovah.

His mission is then briefly described in the words, " He shall bring forth judgment to the Gentiles."   While the statement is a brief one, it is full of suggestiveness in the light of the history of Israel. The purpose for which Israel, the seed of Abraham, was chosen and preserved, was that of blessing to the other nations. Where Israel had failed, the ideal Servant of God would succeed. " He shall bring forth judgment to the Gentiles."

The proclamation then describes the method of the Servant of God. The citation of this passage in the New Testament by Matthew (xii. 20), enables us to understand it more perfectly. In the accomplishment of the purposes of Jehovah, His Servant has first a mission of grace, and then a mission of judgment.

The mission of grace will be characterized by quietness and the absence of all the things which men usually associate with the methods for the establishment of a kingdom. " He shall not cry, nor lift up, nor cause His voice to be heard in the street."   Moreover, during the time of such operation of grace, His method will be that of patience towards His enemies. " A bruised reed shall He not break, and the smoking flax shall He not quench." The bruised reed is the emblem of weakness weakened; and the smoking flax of that in which the principle which will ultimately destroy it, is already at work. During the period of the mission of grace the Servant of God will not hasten the end in either way; He will not break the bruised reed, nor will He extinguish the fire which is already destroying the flax. He will wait patiently.

Beyond the method of grace there will be that of judgment. The prophetic word is, " He shall bring forth judgment in truth." In Matthew's quotation of the prophecy, he interprets it by linking this declaration concerning judgment to that immediately preceding it.

" A bruised reed shall He not break,
 And smoking flax shall He not quench.
 Till He send forth judgment unto victory ";

thus making it evident that in the hour when His method becomes that of judgment, He will break the bruised reed, and quench the smoking flax.

Finally He declares the might of the Servant
of Jehovah in words which put Him into immediate contrast with the enemies with whom
during His mission of grace He is patient, but
whom He will finally destroy in the day of
His judgment. "He will not fail," that is
burn dimly, as does the smoking flax; "nor
be discouraged," that is bruised as is the reed;
"till He have set judgment in the earth."
And just as in dealing with the majesty of
Jehovah the contrast between the false gods
and Jehovah was set forth, so here the enemies
of the Servant of Jehovah are revealed in their
weakness in contrast with Him in His might.

2. *Jehovah and His Servant*

The relation between Jehovah and His
Servant is now declared. All the truth dealt
with in the section setting forth the majesty
of Jehovah, is repeated in condensed form as
He is declared to be the Creator and Sustainer
of the heavens and the earth; and of the people.

His Servant is the "Called" of Jehovah.
He is moreover sustained by Him; and finally
He is appointed, in that He is given in order to
the blessing of the nations. His work amongst
them is that of illumination and deliverance
from all bondage.

The proclamation concerning the Servant ends with the word of Jehovah in which He declares that He will not give His glory to another, nor His praise to graven images. The evidence that His claim to glory is warranted is found in the fact that the things He declares beforehand come to pass.

c. THE RESULTANT APPEAL

The manifesto ends with a section which contains first a song of confidence; secondly a renewed declaration of the purpose of Jehovah; and finally an appeal of the prophet to his people.

1. *The Song of Confidence*

As a result of the vision of the Servant of Jehovah, and of His relationship to Jehovah, the prophet immediately broke forth into a song of confidence, in which he called upon the whole earth to give glory to Jehovah. His appeal is universal. The song must ascend from the end of the earth, and all must take part therein; both such as go down to the sea, and all that is therein; both the islands, and those who dwell thereon. The wilderness, the cities, and the villages of the lands beyond the holy land are to join in the anthem, with the inhabitants of Sela, which is the rock.

The song is to be that which ascribes the glory to Jehovah, and the reason is that He is going forth upon a campaign in which He will be victorious over His enemies.

2. *The Purpose of Jehovah*

The prophetic word now changes into the actual language of Jehovah in which, speaking in the abiding tense of His own existence, He declares that His passion, long restrained in patience, is now to become active in power. All that was said concerning the method of the Servant of God is now spoken by God as of Himself. He has long time holden His peace, been still, and refrained Himself in the method of grace which does not " cry, nor lift up, nor cause His voice to be heard in the street." Now the method will change, and He will cry out, He will gasp and pant, will make waste mountains and hills, and will proceed, as the song of the prophet has declared, as a mighty man for the establishment of judgment.

The issue of this activity of His passion will be the establishment of peace. The needy will find succour; the blind, that is His failing people, will yet be led into the realization of His original purpose; and this succour of the needy will be accompanied by the confusion of all idolaters.

3. *The Prophet's Appeal*

Again the prophetic note changes to one of direct address to the people. The people deaf and blind, are urged to hear and to look. That description of them is then elaborated. They are blind and deaf even though the Divine purpose for them is that they should be servant and messenger of God. They have seen, and yet have not observed.

The law had been given for righteousness' sake, that is in order to their fulfilment of purpose.

But because of their disobedience thereto, they have suffered, and have become a people robbed and spoiled, snared in holes, hid in prison houses, a prey, a spoil.

In view of these things the central appeal is then made in the form of a question, " Who is there among you that will give ear to this? that will hearken and hear for the time to come? "

The manifesto closes with a word about Jacob's suffering. All that which he has passed through, is the punishment of his sin; and in spite of it all, he remains unresponsive.

iii. THE MESSAGES OF JEHOVAH

Following the manifesto, we have a series
of seven messages of Jehovah, each introduced
by the words "Thus saith Jehovah." The
burden of these messages is that of the purpose
of Jehovah for and through His people. They
deal with His perpetual purpose for His people; His present purpose of deliverance; His
power in contrast with that of idols; His
declaration of essential might; His charge to
Cyrus; His ultimate purpose for Israel; and
His purpose for the ends of the earth.

a. HIS PERPETUAL PURPOSE FOR HIS PEOPLE

This message is intended to teach the un-
changeableness of the Divine purpose, and
falls into two parts; the first of which deals
with the fact of the perpetual attitude of Jehovah; while the second declares His present
purpose in the light thereof.

1. *His perpetual Attitude*

The constancy of the attitude of love is
affirmed in promises which gain their force
from the fact that they appeal to deliverances
already wrought. Jehovah first calls to re-

membrance the things of the past, using them
as illustrations of His present purpose. Passing through waters and through rivers, walking through fire, they are to be safe as they
have been safe under similar conditions. As
Egypt, Ethiopia, and Seba have been given
as the price of the ransom of Israel, so men
will still be given for their sake, and peoples
for their life. Thus the past is revealed as
merging into the present.

Because of the abiding presence of Jehovah,
it is affirmed that He will gather His scattered people together; thus the present as-
sures the future.

Then the promise is definitely made of deliverance determined upon, as the result of
which the north must give up, and the south
must not keep back; and all this because of
His past dealing with them, which is summarized by the use of three words, " I have created," " I have formed," " I have made "—the
first suggesting that original activity of God
which is essential causation; the second that
method which, as in the case of the potter
with the clay, is that of sovereignty; the third
being the simplest word which recognizes the
fact that the instrument is the result of the
activity of Jehovah. Thus the future is declared to depend upon the past.

2. *His present Purpose*

Jehovah then declared that His immediate purpose was that the blind people who yet have eyes, and the deaf who still have ears, should be brought forth. The explanation of this figure of speech is found in the prophet's appeal at the close of the manifesto, in which he described the failure of the people of God by declaring their blindness and their dulness of hearing. From this condition it was the present purpose of Jehovah to deliver them, that so they might fulfil His original purpose for them.

Again the nations and the peoples are challenged either to foretell events and justify their foretelling by witnesses, or else to acknowledge that the testimony concerning Jehovah is true. This challenge is a reference to the first movement in the manifesto of Jehovah in which He appealed to the peoples and the idols in the same way.

Having thus challenged the nations and peoples to produce their witnesses, Jehovah proceeded to declare that His people are His witnesses and His servant. The truth to which they were to bear testimony was truth concerning Himself. In order to do this it was necessary that they should know and believe

Him. Upon the basis of such knowledge they were to declare that He is the only God; moreover that He is Jehovah, and that beside Him there is no Saviour. All this He had declared by His dealings with them, and therefore they were to be His witnesses. Therein is a revelation of His original purpose for His people. Israel was intended to be an instrument testifying to truth concerning God.

Finally, notwithstanding the fact that Israel has sadly failed, her ultimate deliverance and fulfilment of vocation as witness is certain because of what God is, and of what He is able to do. The message ends with an announcement and a challenge, " I will work, and who shall reverse it? " This declaration of purpose is rendered powerful by the history of His dealings with His people from the beginning, and by the fact of His abiding presence with them. His purpose is unchanged and unchanging, and His power is equal to the accomplishment thereof.

b. HIS PRESENT PURPOSE OF DELIVERANCE

The second message takes up the theme at the point where the first left it, and describes in greater detail Jehovah's present purpose of deliverance. It consists of a declaration concerning the destruction of their foes; an appeal to Israel; and a promise.

1. *Destruction of Foes*

Again introducing Himself as Jehovah, the Redeemer, the Holy One of Israel, He affirms His determination to destroy their enemies. This He does first by a declaration of His activity, and an affirmation of His purpose. He is already at work, for He has sent to Babylon, and His purpose is the capture and discomfiture of the people thereof.

Because such a declaration might appear unlikely, He repeats the truth concerning Himself that He is Jehovah, the Holy One of Israel, its Creator, and its King.

To this word of self-revelation He adds one which reminds them of His power as it had been manifested in His deliverance of His people from Egypt when He made a way in the sea, and a path in the mighty waters; when He brought low all the power of Egypt, utterly destroying it.

In the midst of this declaration, and for the encouragement of faith, He appealed to past history, which they were in danger of forgetting, or were failing to consider.

The things of the past are to be superseded by the new, which things are illustrated again by historic reference. As in the past He had made a way in the wilderness, and given them rivers in the desert, so will He do again; and all in order that His chosen people, which He had formed for Himself, may set forth His praise.

2. *Appeal to Israel*

The second movement in the message is that of an appeal to Israel, in which their sin is first described. It was first the sin of forgetfulness. In spite of all His purpose for them, and deliverances wrought on their behalf, they had forgotten Him, and had been weary of Him.

This forgetfulness had expressed itself in neglect. This complaint of Jehovah must be considered side by side with other of the prophetic messages. It was not actually true that these people had abandoned the outward observances of worship. There was a sense in which God was weary of their oblations and their sacrifices. The neglect lay deeper, and consisted in the fact that their offerings were those of mechanical observance, rather than the gifts of loving adoration and service.

The final note of their sin was that by sinning they had inflicted injury upon God, making Him to serve, and wearying Him with their iniquities.

Having described the sin, in words full of grace, He uttered the declaration of His pardon, and called them to dealing with Himself, in order to their own justification. There is the most intimate relationship between the declarations "Thou hast made Me to serve with thy sins. . . .," and "I even I, am He that blotteth out thy transgressions for Mine own sake; . . . let us plead together . . . that thou mayest be justified." While sin inflicts injury upon God, the grace that consents to bear the injury makes possible the provision of pardon for the sinner, and opens the way for that dealing with God whereby the sinner may be justified.

The last word of the appeal is one which explains their punishment. All the evil which has happened to them, in which Jacob has been made a curse, and Israel a reviling, is the result of their sin against Him.

3. *The Promise*

The final movement in the message is that of a gracious promise of the outpouring of the Spirit of God, and a description of the blessing and the refreshment and renewal which shall come to Israel, and the consequent influence which will be exerted upon other people.

Jehovah first reminds them of the relationship existing between His people and Himself. He speaks of Jacob as His servant, of Israel as His chosen; again declaring that Israel owes its existence to Him, and that He will still help. Upon the basis of this relationship He utters the great " Fear not," and proceeds to declare His purpose of blessing; first under the figure of water, and of streams upon the thirsty land, and upon the dry ground; and then definitely in the promise of His Spirit upon the people of His love. As the grass springs when the rains fall, and as the willows grow by the water-courses, so will His people prosper and flourish as the result of the outpouring of His Spirit.

As the result of this renewal of His own people, blessing will flow to others. The revelation of Jehovah through the prosperity of

His people will constrain others to submission to Him, who in turn will bear His name, and share their privileges; all of which is according to His first and perpetual purpose for them, and through them for the world.

c. HIS POWER COMPARED WITH THAT OF IDOLS

The third message is one in which Jehovah compares His power with that of idols. It falls into three parts. The first is a declaration that Jehovah is the only God; the second sets forth the folly of idolatry; while the third is again an appeal to Israel.

1. *Jehovah the only God*

Re-affirming His relation to His people as King and Redeemer, Jehovah declares Himself to be the last, and that beside Him there is no God.

These facts are demonstrated as He is seen knowing, declaring, and appointing; in all of which He is alone, having neither rival nor competitor.

Because these things are so, the people are appealed to, not to fear. They themselves are the witnesses of the truth of the declarations.

2. *The Folly of Idolatry*

Then follows a remarkable passage setting forth the folly of idolatry. The people who make a graven image are themselves vanity or confusion.

Their work is unprofitable, and they, as
the witnesses of their gods, are blind and
ignorant; and therefore are not ashamed. Attention is fastened upon the unutterable folly
of the image-maker by the question, "Who
hath fashioned a god, or molten a graven
image that is profitable for nothing?" The
emphasis of the question is on this first word
"who." The vision of the unprofitable idol
is in itself a revelation of the vanity of the
idol-maker.

With fine satire the whole process of the
making of an idol is then described. Catch-
ing up the thought suggested by the inquiry
"Who," it is declared that of such an one even
his fellows shall be ashamed.

In demonstration of this, the process of the
making is described. Men put their strength
into the fashioning of an idol of metal, and
as the result of the exercise of strength, they
become hungry, and strength fails, but there
is none to feed. Others work in wood, making
gods with their own tools after the likeness
of a man, whose only ability, when made, is
that of remaining in the house. These gods
of wood are made out of the chosen trees
of the forest. The process of the nourishing
and choosing of the tree is described, and the
satire of the description consists in the fact

that the making of a god is the last activity.
Of the tree, man makes a fire to warm himself
and to roast his meat, and when his own needs
have been supplied by his own activity, with
what remains of the tree he makes a god which
he worships, and asks it to deliver him.

The madness of it all is that idol-makers
are so blind that they are not conscious of
the folly of their procedure. This blindness
is the most appalling nemesis of idolatry.

The contrast between Jehovah, the first and
the last, knowing, declaring, appointing; and
the idols made by men, unable to help men,
is graphic.

3. *The Appeal to Israel*

The message ends with an appeal to Israel
to remember. The appeal is based first upon
the fact of the relationship of Israel to God;
and secondly upon the fact that God has not
forgotten Israel.

The second word of appeal is introduced by
the declaration of grace, that Jehovah has
blotted out transgressions and sins, and urges
His people to return to Him, because He has
redeemed them.

The final note is that of the song of redemption. The heavens and the earth, the

mountains, the forest, and every tree are called
to the exercise of praise because Jehovah hath
redeemed Jacob, and will glorify Himself in
Israel. This message dealing with the power
of Jehovah as compared with that of idols
ends with a joyful recognition that His purpose of peace will ultimately be accomplished
as His own people are restored to the fulfilment of their true function in His economy.

d. HIS DECLARATION OF MIGHT.   xliv. 24-28

1. *The backward Look.*   24

   α. *The Relation to Israel.*
   β. *The Might of Creation.*
   γ. *In Loneliness.*

2. *The continuous Fact.*   25-27

   α. *Frustrating Evil.*   25
   β. *Confirming Good.*   26a
   γ. *Accomplishing Purpose.*   26b, 27

3. *The immediate Action.*   28

   α. *Of Cyrus.*
   β. *Of Jerusalem.*
   γ. *Of the Temple.*

d. HIS DECLARATION OF MIGHT

The fourth message is a brief one, but full of strength and beauty as it majestically sets forth the might of Jehovah in three movements; the first of which is of the nature of a backward look; the second dealing with the continuous fact; and the last declaring the immediate action.

1. *The backward Look*

Again reminding His people of His relation to them as Redeemer· and Creator, Jehovah declares His might in the material realm. He is the Maker of all things, and that in the loneliness of His power. The illustrations are inclusive, and are those of the heavens stretched forth, and the earth spread abroad.

2. *The continuous Fact*

Continuing, He claims that His might is manifested in His government in the moral realm. He frustrates the operations of evil, and confirms the intentions of good. Moreover, it proceeds to the accomplishment of purpose, and that in spite of all appearances to the contrary. Jerusalem desolate, shall be inhabited. The cities of Judah destroyed, shall be built. The forces that oppose will be overcome, the deep will be dry, and the rivers also.

3. *The immediate Action*

The last word in the declaration of might brings the thought back to that which is to be immediately accomplished in the days to which the prophet is looking on. This Jehovah, powerful in the material realm, governing in the moral, is moving forward towards the restoration of His people by the appointment of Cyrus who will perform His pleasure; and by declaring His purpose that Jerusalem shall be built, and the foundation of the temple shall be laid.

e. HIS CHARGE TO CYRUS

The fifth of these messages of Jehovah consists of His charge to Cyrus. The first part is an introductory word presenting the man; then follows the charge itself; and finally a solemn word of protest is uttered against objections to the Divine choice of the instrument.

1. *Introduction*

In the last message dealing with the might of Jehovah its immediate activity was indicated in the declaration that Cyrus would act as Jehovah's shepherd, performing all his pleasure. In the present message Cyrus is first presented as the anointed of Jehovah. He is seen as an instrument for the accomplishment of the Divine purpose; and in order thereto he is anointed, appointed, and sustained to subdue nations. In order to this Jehovah declares His purpose of preparing the way by loosing the loins of kings, that is, filling them with fear, and opening doors before him.

2. *The Charge*

The charge to Cyrus is introduced by promises which are intended to be his strength

in the carrying out of the Divine purpose.
The promises are that Jehovah will go before him to make the way plain, breaking
down all obstacles, and that He will give him
the spoil of his victories; and the purpose of
all this action on the part of Jehovah is that
Cyrus may know that He is Jehovah.

Cyrus is thus to be used of God for the
sake of Jacob and Israel. Moreover even
though Cyrus does not know God, He will
gird him, in order that the wider world from
sunrise to sunset may know that Jehovah is
God, and beside Him there is none else.

The immediate charge ends with the declaration of the ability of Jehovah first in the
material world, in that He forms the light
and creates darkness; and secondly in the
moral world, in that He makes peace and
creates evil, that is calamity. The whole
movement of the activity of Jehovah is then
figuratively set forth. Righteousness is to de-
scend from above, and the earth is to open
that she may be fruitful in salvation. Thus it
is declared to Cyrus, that God is the source
of righteousness; and that it is His power
which over-rules the affairs of earth, so that
the kingdom of heaven which is righteousness,
is set thereon.

3. *Protest against Objections*

The last section of the charge to Cyrus is of the nature of a protest against objections. The idea of the employment by God of a man outside the covenant, and of another nation, was entirely contrary to the pride and prejudice of the Hebrew people. The same attitude of mind is discovered and dealt with more fully in the prophecy of Habakkuk. Here there is no argument in defence of the action of Jehovah other than that of the assertion of His sovereign right. Thus is revealed the folly and uselessness of rebellion in this matter.

The folly is illustrated by the figure of the clay in revolt against the potter, and of the child in rebellion against its parents. It is finally stated directly by words challenging the attitude of those raising objection. If, as some suppose, the words of Jehovah here should be read as though they were questions, " Do ye ask Me of the things that are to come? Concerning My sons, and concerning the work of My hands, do ye command Me? " the intention of protest is evident. If, on the other hand, we are to read the passage as it appears in our translations as an imperative, it is still evident by the illustrations already referred to, that the imperative is satirical rather than of the nature of a positive command. For men to raise objections to Jehovah's choice and use of instruments is as foolish as for clay to criticise the potter, or for a child to protest against its begetting and its birth.

The uselessness of such protest is revealed in the light of the original right of Jehovah, based upon the fact that He is Creator; and finally it is declared in the light of His present action, and of the fact that the method and the purpose of that action are what they are. The method is that Jehovah raises Cyrus in righteousness, and His purpose is that Cyrus shall build His city, and let His exiles go free, and that not for price or for reward.

This whole charge to Cyrus is a revelation of the facts of the actuality and perpetuity of the Divine government, not only over His own people, but over the whole world for the sake of His people, and over His people for the sake of the whole world. If they fail, He will lay His hand upon a man of another nation, and lead him on a campaign of conquest in order to the accomplishment of His purpose, and the restoration of His failing people.

The central teaching of the charge may be said to find clearest expression in the words

addressed to Cyrus, " I have surnamed thee
though thou hast not known Me. . . . I will
gird thee though thou hast not known Me."
While men may frustrate and postpone for
a period the accomplishment of the Divine
purpose; while instead of the preparation of
straight paths for God, men may by rebellion
compel the necessity for the circuitous route,
they can neither dethrone Him nor prevent
His ultimate triumph.   He compels all men
and all movements to contribute towards that
end.

f. HIS ULTIMATE PURPOSE FOR ISRAEL

Immediately following the charge to Cyrus, the sixth message re-affirms the ultimate purpose of Jehovah for His own people.

That purpose is first the submission of the peoples who by their labour and their merchandise will contribute to the prosperity of Israel. This they will do in complete submission. The inspiring cause of such submission will be the discovery by these people of the fact that God is in the midst of His own, and that beside Him there is no God.

The words immediately following this declaration concerning the submission of the peoples, " Verily Thou art a God that hidest Thyself, O God of Israel, the Saviour," constitute a parenthesis. Whether they are the words of the people as they come into the place of submission to Jehovah, or whether they are the words of the prophet is open to question. I should personally be inclined to treat them as the words of the prophet, an exclamation of the recognition of the mystery of the Divine method, and an admission of the wisdom thereof as demonstrated by the final issue. In that case they constitute a further answer to the folly of those who protest against the choice of such an instrument as Cyrus.

Such submission of the peoples will be the occasion of the ultimate shame of idol-makers, for they will go into confusion together.

In immediate contrast to the shame of such, Israel will be saved with an everlasting salvation, and will neither be ashamed nor confounded.

Again in this picture of His ultimate purpose for Israel His larger intention of blessing to the distant nations is recognized and plainly declared. In Him alone there is salvation for His own people and all the peoples. Apart from Him there is nothing but shame and confusion.

g. HIS PURPOSE FOR THE ENDS OF THE EARTH

As in the charge to Cyrus, His larger purpose of Self-revelation to all, from the rising of the sun and from the west, was declared, the last of the seven messages deals with that purpose particularly. In this message there are three movements, in the first of which there is declared the original purpose in creation; then the purpose of the seed of Jacob; and finally the call to the peoples based upon these facts.

1. *The Purpose of Creation*

Again affirming His own sovereignty, and that beside Him there is none else, Jehovah declares that He formed the earth and made it, that He established it and created it not a waste, but that it might be inhabited. All creation prior to man is thus set in relationship to him. In all the processes of the Divine activity man was in view, and the creation of the earth was but the preparation of a home for him.

2. *The Purpose of the Seed of Jacob*

Having thus created the earth and its inhabitants, He did not leave them without witness. His speech had not been in secret in a land of darkness. As the purpose of the creation of the earth was not that it should be a waste, so His choice of the seed of Jacob was not that it should be a waste. His method with men is that of speaking and declaring; and the purpose for which the seed of Jacob was chosen was that they should constitute an instrument through which He might reveal Himself.

3. *The Call to the Peoples*

On the foundation of these assertions of purpose in original creation, and in the seed of Jacob, the call to the nations is uttered.

The declarations which immediately follow suggest to the peoples a comparison of idols with Jehovah. In the light of all that had been said in previous messages concerning the method by which men make idols, and their uselessness, it is now affirmed that such as carry the wood of the graven image, and pray unto a god that cannot save, are without knowledge. In immediate contrast the peoples are called to take counsel together, and to recognize that the God Who has persistently and from ancient time showed and revealed these things of righteousness is the only God; and that He is a just God and a Saviour.

In view of these things the great invitation of infinite grace is uttered to the ends of the earth as they are called to look to Jehovah and so to find salvation. This invitation is emphasized by the declaration of Jehovah's determination that every knee must bow to Him, and to Him every tongue must swear. It is within His purpose that all shall come to Him in submission and in confession. The method of the acceptation of this invitation is foretold as the recognition that righteousness and strength are to be found only in Jehovah. Through that recognition men will come to Him.

The final word of the last of these messages is the declaration that in Jehovah all the seed of Israel shall be justified and shall glory; and this word, interpreted in the light of the teaching of the messages, includes the thought that His purposes of illumination and blessing for the ends of the earth must inevitably be realized.

iv. THE MIGHT OF JEHOVAH

The fourth movement in this section of the prophecy celebrates the might of Jehovah, as manifested in the downfall of Babylon. The message falls into two parts; the fall of Babylon determined; and the fall of Babylon described.

a. THE FALL OF BABYLON DETERMINED

In dealing with the Divine determination to destroy Babylon the prophet first contrasts the idols of Babylon with Jehovah; then utters the challenge of Jehovah; and finally declares His counsel.

1. *The Contrast*

The message opens with a graphic picture of the idols being hurried away for safety, carried upon beasts of burden. Bel and Nebo, the chief of the Babylonian deities, are represented as crouching in the attitude of weakness and of fear. The idols are seen placed upon the beasts. With infinite scorn the prophet describes them as " the things that ye carried about." These false gods, so far from being able to deliver those who trusted in them from captivity, are themselves carried by the people into captivity. The central thought of the picture is that of gods that have to be carried.

In immediate contrast the prophet presents Jehovah as the One Who carried His people. This He has done from birth, and this He declares He will do until old age. There is again an affirmation of that so often insisted upon, that He is the Creator, and the corollary is insisted upon anew, that He will carry, and will deliver.

2. *The Challenge*

In the light of that contrast Jehovah utters His challenge, asking to whom they will liken Him, make Him equal, or compare Him.

The only answer possible to the idolater would be that of suggesting his god. Therefore the challenge ends with a description of the idol, which shows at once the unutterable folly of any such comparison. The idol is made. It has to be carried, and when set in its place is unable to move. When one cries unto it, it can neither answer nor save.

All this sets forth the sin of Babylon, and opens the way for the declaration of the counsel of Jehovah which has determined upon the destruction of Babylon.

3. *The Counsel*

Of this the first word is addressed to the transgressors, that is, those among the people of God who are in rebellion against Him; in all probability those to whom the prophet had before referred, who protested against the idea of the use of Cyrus as an instrument of the Divine procedure. These are called upon to remember first the former things which had demonstrated the fact that Jehovah was God and that there was none beside. This had been shown in the fact of His "declaring the end from the beginning"; "saying, My counsel shall stand"; "calling the ravenous bird from the east." He had announced what He would do, and this very calling of Cyrus, contrary to all which the transgressors thought fitting, was in itself evidence of His power. In the hearing of these transgressors the affirmation is then made, "I have spoken, I will also bring it to pass."

The second word concerning the counsel is addressed to the stout-hearted, that is, to the actual enemies of Jehovah who are called upon to hearken to Him. To them He affirms His determination to bring near His righteousness, to place salvation in Zion, all of which constitutes the declaration of His determination to destroy Babylon.

b. THE FALL OF BABYLON DESCRIBED

The prophecy is now addressed to Babylon itself, and describes its judgment in language full of force and beauty. That description is fourfold, and deals with the process which beginning with degradation, proceeds through disgrace and desolation, to complete destruction.

1. *Degradation*

First the degradation of the city is foretold. From the place of delicacy she is to pass to that of grinding and of shame. The city that has claimed to be the " virgin daughter of Babylon " characterized by all the refinements of luxury, is to sit in the dust without a throne. Nay more, she is to enter into the experience of slavery and of shame, and the Agent of the degradation is Jehovah Himself Who declares, " I will take vengeance, and will make truce with no man." The prophet was careful to explain that this is the word of Jehovah Himself, as he described Him by the names and titles which he had made use of in the messages which have been considered; " the Redeemer, Jehovah of hosts, the Holy One of Israel."

2. *Disgrace*

The place to which Babylon comes is moreover to be a place of disgrace. She is to sit silent in the darkness, and no more to be called "the lady of kingdoms." She who has borne that title because of her supremacy over many peoples, is to sit without speech and without light in disgrace.

The sin of which this disgrace is the punishment the prophet declared in words attributed to Jehovah Himself. He had been wroth with His own people, and had made Babylon the instrument of their punishment. Babylon had made use of the opportunity to crush and oppress the people of God, showing them no mercy, and laying the yoke heavily upon them.

Moreover this she had done in a pride of heart, without compassion, and in forgetfulness of the inevitable nemesis of such action toward another people.

3. *Desolation*

Continuing, the prophet showed that the disgrace will issue in desolation. The city given to pleasure, full of pride, pride which expressed itself in language which can only be used accurately by God, " I am, and there is none else beside Me "; pride which had declared that the city could never be moved, and never know sorrow; is to be rendered childless and widowed in a day, and that in spite of her sorceries, and the abundance of the enchantments in which she had placed her trust.

In dealing with the desolation the prophet finally declared the relation between this pride and punishment. Babylon had trusted in her wickedness, had said that none saw her.

By reason of her wisdom and her knowledge she had been perverted until she had used the offending words, " I am, and there is none else beside me." Therefore said the prophet, evil would come upon her, and mischief fall upon her; and these things should come in such fashion that Babylon in her blindness would be unable to detect the first beginnings of judgment.

4. *Destruction*

Finally the prophet declared that the judgment would be the utter destruction of the city. He challenged the city to stand up against the processes of the Divine judgment; and called upon her to let her astrologers, and stargazers, and monthly prognosticators, save her from the threatening peril.

All would be of no avail. The fire would destroy them as stubble. It would be a fire, not for comfort, but for burning; and so terrible would be the destruction, that those who had trafficked with the city from her youth would abandon her.

The last word to the city which had put her trust in idols, in enchantments, in all wickedness, is " there shall be none to save thee."

v. The Mercy of Jehovah

The last section of the division dealing with the purpose of peace is of the nature of an appeal to the people, and deals with the mercy of Jehovah. It describes Jehovah's methods, gives an illustration, re-affirms His purpose, and utters the final word.

a. JEHOVAH'S METHODS

In demanding the attention of the people the prophet recognized the fact of their failure. The message was evidently addressed to the remnant; and even that remnant had failed. He recognized the Divine purpose for the whole nation when he spoke of the house of Jacob, called by the name of Israel; but he also recognized that such purpose was being fulfilled in a remnant, when he described the house of Jacob as having come forth out of the waters of Judah. This remnant of the tribe of Judah whom the prophet had in view, he addressed as the house of Jacob only because he saw how that remnant was the medium through which the Divine purpose was being carried forward towards its fulfilment in the person of the servant of Jehovah. Nevertheless the remnant was in itself a fail-

ing one; swearing by the name of Jehovah,
making mention of the God of Israel, but not
in truth, that is with inward sincerity; nor
in righteousness, that is with outward loyalty.
Nevertheless they called themselves of the holy
city, and stayed themselves upon the God of
Israel. They failed, but there was still the
principle of faith manifest in their attitudes,
and to that Jehovah made His appeal, and
through that He moved forward towards the
accomplishment of His purpose.

Having thus summoned this remnant to attention, the prophet proceeded to declare that
the method of Jehovah had been that of
prophecy and performance. The former
things He had declared from of old. Here the
reference could not have been to Cyrus, for
whether near or distant, he was still seen as
approaching. It was rather a reference to the
continued method of God with this people—
that of prediction. The things He had foretold He had always accomplished.

His reason for adopting this method of prediction was that of the obstinacy and defiant
rebellion of His people. The fact of the foretelling of events by the prophets of Jehovah
made it impossible for them to attribute the
events to idols. As had been the case with
regard to former things, so now it was with

regard to new things. Things which the people had not known, of which they had not heard, and concerning which they could not say, I knew them, were now being revealed to them; and that again because of their habitual treachery, and their constant transgression.

The whole point of this declaration of the method of Jehovah is that of insistence upon the predictive element in the prophetic teaching, as showing that all the processes were under the government of God. The prophet was careful to show that these things foretold were immediately created, and not from of old; that is to say, the events referred to were not merely the natural outcome of human forces, but would result from the will of Jehovah, of which His word is ever the accomplishing agent.

The abiding purpose of God, that His name should be glorified, was finally declared as the reason of His mercy. For the sake of that name His anger was deferred, and His chosen people were not destroyed. The refinement of His people cannot be accomplished by the process of material fire, as in the case of silver, but by that of mental and spiritual fire in the furnace of affliction. Through all such processes Jehovah was preparing the instrument

for the fulfilling of His will, and the glorifying
of His name.

b. AN ILLUSTRATION

The message then proceeded to give an illustration of this method of prophecy and performance—first introducing Jehovah by names
and titles, and then by recounting deeds of
power which set Him anew before the mind
in His glory and majesty. " I am He," " I am
the first, I also am the last," are declarations
characterized by simplicity of language and
sublimity of conception. Jehovah is the Creator, at Whose bidding all the things of the
earth and the heaven stand up together.

Again challenging them as to which of them
has declared these things, that is, in the sense
of prediction, Jehovah's choice of an instrument for the doing of His will is declared.
His servant is seen as one whose work it is
to perform the Divine pleasure on Babylon,
and that because he is called by Jehovah, and
brought by Him, in order to the accomplishment of His purpose. Whereas the first fulfilment in history of this prediction was in the
person of Cyrus, its ultimate and perfect and
spiritual fulfilment never came until the coming of that perfect One of Whom all prior to

Him had been but imperfect foreshadowings.

Again the prophet challenged those to whom
his appeal was made to come near and hear as
Jehovah declared that He had not spoken in
secret, that is, that He had distinctly foretold;
and moreover, that through all the processes
He had been present. This declaration ends
with words that are very remarkable. " And
now the Lord God hath sent Me; and His
Spirit." These words are undoubtedly the
words of God, and yet they are words of One
Who speaks as being sent, and of being sent
in fellowship with the Spirit of God. This
affirmation is not only obscure, but without
meaning, if it is made to refer only to the
coming of Cyrus; whereas it is full of illumination if it is understood of Him Who, being with
God, was God; but Who ever spoke of Himself
as sent by God; and Whose whole life and
ministry in the world was one of co-operation
with the Spirit of God.

c. JEHOVAH'S PURPOSE

Again, the purpose of God is declared to be
that of the profit and peace of His people.
He is Jehovah, the Redeemer and the Holy
One of Israel. He is Jehovah, the God of
Israel, teaching to profit, Whose command-

ments being obeyed, peace as a river results, and righteousness as the waves of the sea. This purpose of peace is determined upon by God; and the prophet, with his vision still occupied with the future, cried to the people to go forth of Babylon, because Jehovah had redeemed His servant Jacob. He Who in the past had led them through the deserts without thirst, causing waters to flow from the rock for them, was still their Redeemer.

d. FINAL WORD

This first division dealing with the purpose of peace ends with the solemn affirmation that there is no peace to the wicked. Thus while the purpose of God has been clearly shown to be that of peace, His people were solemnly warned that this purpose could never be realized in their experience while they persisted in wickedness.

The picture presented to the mind by this first division is that of the chosen people of God under circumstances of danger and of difficulty almost amounting to desolation. The prophetic word to them is pre-eminently one of comfort. That comfort is based upon the fact of the majesty and might and mercy of Jehovah. He is seen by the prophet in all

His essential and demonstrated glory, and by comparison with Him the weakness and vanity of idols is manifest. The burden of the prophet is that of the manifesto of Jehovah, wherein He affirms His purpose of blessing, and claims as evidence of His power, the fact of the foretelling of events. At the centre of that manifesto is the proclamation concerning the Servant Who is to accomplish all His will.

In view of that proclamation a series of messages to His people are delivered by the prophet, and finally His might is revealed in the predicted downfall of Babylon, and His mercy in His purpose of redemption for His people. Thus all the teaching of the division centres in the prediction concerning the Servant of Jehovah. The next division presents that Servant in fuller detail, and shows how the purpose of peace will be realized through the Prince of peace.

II. THE PRINCE OF PEACE

This section, in which the Prince of peace is most clearly revealed, falls into two distinct parts. The Servant of God is seen, first sustained through suffering; and secondly singing in triumph. As the prophet described this Servant of God, his reference sometimes seems to have been to the nation of Israel, sometimes to Cyrus, and yet constantly to One differing from, and greater than either. It is impossible to those who have the New Testament, and who believe in its authority, to fail to recognize the Messianic value of this section. The principal element of the prophetic utterances is that of the principles of the Divine activity; and these are seen partially fulfilled in different ways, but all finally fulfilled in the one Servant of God.

i. SUSTAINED THROUGH SUFFERING

In presenting the picture of the Servant of God sustained through suffering, the prophet dealt first with Jehovah's call, and secondly with His Servant's answer.

a. JEHOVAH'S CALL

The call of Jehovah to His Servant has three movements dealing with the values of that call; first, as to His Servant; secondly, as to Zion; and thirdly as to Jehovah Himself.

1. *As to His Servant*

As in the case of the manifesto of Jehovah in the previous division, the isles and the peoples are called upon to listen and hearken to the declaration of the call of the Servant of God. It is chronicled in the words of the Servant Himself, Who declares the fact of His call, first affirming His ordination to service from His birth, and then recognizing how perfectly He was equipped for His work, which work however was that of an instrument in the hand of Jehovah. Thus created, equipped, and kept for service, the word of Jehovah described Him as "Israel, in Whom I will be glorified," thus placing Him in immediate and striking contrast to the national Israel which had so grievously failed.

The reply of the Servant declares the comparative failure of His mission, but nevertheless affirms His confidence that His judgment is with Jehovah, and His recompense with His God. This apparent failure produces no discouragement because He recognizes that in the hand of Jehovah He is an instrument for the accomplishment of a Divine purpose, and in that fact He rests.

In answer to that word of confidence the Servant, still speaking, tells of the confirmation of His call by Jehovah. Again referring to the fact that He was appointed to service from birth, He does so even more emphatically in that He no longer speaks of Himself as called from birth, but as formed from birth to the fulfilment of His office.

The first purpose is the bringing again of Jacob to Jehovah, and the gathering to Him of Israel. This is immediately followed by an explanation which in the Revised Version is fittingly placed in parenthesis, in which the Servant of God recognizes the honour conferred upon Him, and the fact that God is His strength.

The first purpose, of blessing to Jacob, was however too light a thing for Him, and He was destined for world-wide influence, to be " a light to the Gentiles," and " My salvation unto the end of the earth." That the pathway of the Servant must be that of suffering proceeding to triumph is then explicitly stated. This is the appointment of Jehovah Who is again, as so often before, described as the Redeemer of Israel, and His Holy One. The Servant of God will be despised of men, abhorred of the nation, a Servant of rulers; but kings and princes will arise and wor-

ship as the result of His appointment by Jehovah.

The mission of the Servant of God is then
described in the language of Jehovah Himself.
This mission is first referred to as the answer
of Jehovah to His Servant, the truth involved
being that of the perfect conformity of the
desire of the Servant of Jehovah with the purposes of Jehovah Himself. The sustaining
power of Jehovah is declared. In the acceptable time, that is, at the right moment, in
the fulness of time, according to the foreordi-
nation of God, Jehovah answers the desire of
His Servant, in a day of salvation; in the day
in which, in fellowship with Jehovah, His
Servant accomplishes the work of salvation,
Jehovah is His Helper, and through all the
process Jehovah preserves Him. The outcome
of this is the ability of the Servant to carry
out the purposes of Jehovah, and this is declared in the promise that He is given as a
covenant to the people. The results of this
are the establishment of the earth, and the
bringing of the people into the inheritance of
desolate heritages.

In language full of poetic beauty the work
is then described. Those who are bound are to
be set at liberty, and those who are in darkness
are to pass into the light. They are to feed

and find pasture on places hitherto barren. They are neither to hunger nor thirst, neither to be smitten by mirage nor sun, because they are to be led by Jehovah Himself. His mission will moreover result in blessing to those who are afar off. They are to be gathered from the distant places. In a burst of song the description of the mission ends, and the reason of the song is that Jehovah hath comforted His people, and will have compassion upon His afflicted.

2. *As to Zion*

The call of Jehovah is now given in its bearing upon Zion.

Zion complains that Jehovah has forsaken her, and the Lord, her sovereign Ruler, has forgotten her.

The reply to this complaint is in the nature of an affirmation of His unfailing love, and the certainty of her deliverance. The supreme illustration of human affection is suggested in the question, " Can a woman forget her sucking child, that she should not have compassion on the son of her womb? " Nothing can be more unlikely than such forgetfulness, and yet, in order that the constancy of the Divine love may be affirmed, it is admitted

that she may. Zion is graven upon the palms
of Jehovah's hands, and notwithstanding her
present ruin and desolation, He sees her walls.
His love is an unfailing love. The certainty
of her deliverance is then declared. Those
who have destroyed her, and made her waste,
shall be expelled; and her children and the
peoples will gather themselves to her, and they
shall be her glory. The places now waste and
desolate shall be too strait for those who shall
crowd to her in the day of her restoration;
and all this in spite of that present experience
in which the city is bereft of children, and is
seen desolate as a widow, left alone. The deliverance is certain, and its glory will be such
as to surprise Zion, and make her exclaim,
" Who hath begotten me these? "

3. *As to Jehovah*

Having thus dealt with the call of Jehovah
as to His Servant, and as to Zion; the last
movement describes it as to Jehovah Himself.
This description is first an answer to the inquiry of Zion as to whence the children have
come who crowd to her in the day of restoration. It is He Who will lift up His hand to
the nations, and His ensign to the peoples,
and these shall come to Zion bringing back

her sons and her daughters. Kings and queens shall be the nursing fathers and mothers of the bereft and desolate city, and shall yield allegiance to her.

The promise is so great and gracious that an exclamation of surprise and of wonder escaped the lips of the prophet, " Shall the prey be taken from the mighty, or the lawful captives be delivered? " and the answer of Jehovah is clear that these things will be accomplished because He will act in contention with, and judgment against, all those who oppress Zion, so that all flesh will know that He is the Saviour, the Redeemer, and Mighty One of Jacob. Such is His description, concerning her.

Returning again to the complaint of Zion that she is forsaken of Jehovah, and forgotten of her Lord, He charges her to produce the bill of divorcement, or to find creditors to Whom He has sold her. The two great figures of relationship so often occurring in the prophetic writings are here recognized, the first being that of the ancient people of God as betrothed to Him, and the second that of their being His possession. With a fine irony, which is nevertheless the irony of unfailing love, He demands evidences that He has divorced her, or sold her to creditors.

He then proceeds to give His own answer
to the challenge as He declares first the real
reason for that desolation which finds them
in captivity, and put away from fellowship
with Him. The reason is that of their own
iniquities, and their own transgressions.
Turning the complaint against them, He inquires, "Wherefore, when I came, was there
no man? when I called was there none to
answer?" It is not that He had forsaken
them, but that they had forsaken Him. They
had broken the covenant, and failed to respond
to the call of His love. Nevertheless, in spite
of all this, His love has not failed, and He
demands, "Is Mine hand shortened at all, that
it cannot redeem? or have I no power to deliver?" and He answers this inquiry by reminding them of His power as it had been
manifested in their own history, both in the
way of deliverance and the way of judgment.

The whole movement of this call of Jehovah
is full of the revelation of His grace and His
power, and fastens attention upon the fact
that He will accomplish His purposes of peace
through the One Whom He has called and
ordained. The call of the Servant is first re-
corded, and ends with the wonderful picture
of the glorious restoration which will ultimately result therefrom.

In circumstances of desolation Zion is filled with despair, and her complaint Jehovah answers first by the affirmation of His unfailing love, and then by the proclamation of His determination to deliver; and He denies His own unfaithfulness to covenant, as He reveals the reason of all the suffering through which His people have passed to be that of their sin.

b. HIS SERVANT'S ANSWER

This section records the answer of the Servant to the call of Jehovah, and falls into three parts. The first of these is an expression of His consecration to suffering; the second describes the ministry of suffering; while the third deals with the completion of suffering.

1. *Consecration to Suffering*

This paragraph is full of value, as it reveals the attitude of the ideal Servant of God, and thus reveals the secrets of His endurance, and of His ultimate triumph. It first tells of His consecration to the work, and then affirms His courage.

α. His Consecration

The consecration of the Servant of God is the act of God, to which act the Servant responds in dedication. Two brief words declare the method of that consecration. " The Lord God hath given Me the tongue of them that are taught," " the Lord God hath opened Mine ear."

The first reveals the fact that the message which the ideal Servant is to deliver is one

which He has received from God.   Moreover,
it is a message in harmony with the constant
thought of this division of the prophecy, that
of comfort; for its purpose is the sustenance of
such as are weary.   The phrase, " the tongue
of them that are taught," is a very suggestive
one, showing, as we have already indicated,
that the message delivered by the Servant of
God is one which He has received from God.
The patience with which God imparts His
message is suggested by the declaration, " He
wakeneth morning by morning."   The first act
of consecration to service on the part of God
is this of imparting the truth in such measure
and in such form as are necessary for the
accomplishment of His purpose.

The second fact in that consecration is expressed in the word, " The Lord God hath
opened Mine ear," which means far more than
that He makes His Servant listen.   That has
already been stated in connection with the
declaration of consecration by the imparted
word.   It suggests the idea that God makes
His Servant willing to hear, in order to declare
things which will bring Him into conflict with
those to whom His message is to be delivered.
This is seen in the immediate declaration, " I
was not rebellious, neither turned away backward."   The word " opened " here must not

be confused with one occurring in Psalm xl. 6. That word means digged, or pierced, or bored; and in that connection has reference to the ceremony of the boring of the ear against the door-post in token of submission. Here the thought is that of consecration by constraint of the will to listen to whatever Jehovah has to say.

Such listening will compel speech, which will provoke opposition, and knowing this, the Servant of God dedicates Himself in answer to the consecration by consenting to the suffering involved, expressing this dedication in the words, " I gave My back to the smiters, and My cheeks to them that plucked off the hair: I hid not My face from shame and spitting."

β. His Courage

The courage of the Servant of God is the immediate result of His consecration by God, and finds expression in declarations which show that He proceeds upon His way in the evident assurance of fellowship with God.

In a ministry in the midst of opposition, He is equipped for courageous loyalty to the purpose of God by assurance that He will not be ashamed, because He knows that in such an attitude the Lord God will help Him.

In a ministry which must be one of conflict against the adversary, in full assurance of His ability to overcome, He challenges the adversary to come near, because He knows that the Lord God will help Him, and His ministry therefore will be one of victory with God. Thus in the consciousness and power of an intimate fellowship with God, His Servant faces the pathway of obedience, knowing that it must be a pathway of suffering, but knowing also that its ultimate end must be that of triumph.

2. *The Ministry of Suffering*

The Servant of God thus consecrated to
suffering, and full of courage in the contempla-
tion of it, enters upon a ministry of suffering.
This section which embodies the principles and
reveals the method of the ministry of the one
great Servant of God Who is ever in view,
does nevertheless peculiarly apply to the ministry of the prophet himself among a people
in days of darkness and desolation. In this
ministry there is first a word which separates
the people into two camps; then three messages delivered to the faithful; and finally
three to the afflicted.

α. *The Separation*

The word separating the people, divides between those who are faithful to Jehovah, and
those who, turning their back upon Him, walk
in the way of their own counsels.

The faithful are described as in circumstances of darkness, but nevertheless walking
in the fear of the Lord, and in obedience to
the voice of His Servant.

On the other hand are such as are also in
darkness, but they are attempting to create
a light by fires which they have kindled. Those

true to God are commanded to trust in the
name of Jehovah, and stay upon God. Those
seeking to walk in the light of their own fires
are told that they shall lie down in sorrow.

Having thus uttered the separating word,
the messages which follow are to those who
fear the Lord, and obey the voice of His
Servant.

β. *Messages to the Faithful*

These messages are all calculated to cheer
and comfort those who are in the midst of
circumstances of darkness. The first is a call
to courage; the second is the cry of courage;
and the third declares the cause of courage.

The Call to Courage

In order to inspire the hearts of those who
walk in the darkness with courage, the prophet
called them to look back, to look on, and to
look around; in each case in order that they
might observe the working of Jehovah.

The backward look must remind them that
their origin was in God. Their father Abraham was called by God, and by Him blessed
and made many. The introduction of the
name of Sarah emphasized the fact of the

Divine power as it reminded them that the whole nation resulted from an activity beyond the natural. Therefore the prophet spoke of the rock whence they were hewn, which was not Abraham, but Jehovah. The vision of Jehovah in the backward look produced the affirmation, " Jehovah hath comforted Zion," and that in spite of the fact that at the moment the circumstances were those of sorrow and of desolation.

The onward look therefore must be one of confidence, for righteousness had not been destroyed, and must inevitably triumph in the salvation of the peoples. The heavens and the earth will vanish away, but the salvation of Jehovah will be for ever, and His righteousness cannot be abolished.

Therefore the look around, even though it be upon darkness and upon the hatred and opposition of men opposed to Jehovah, cannot produce fear; for those who know righteousness, and in whose heart is the law of God, know also that His enemies must be destroyed, and His purposes of righteousness and salvation fulfilled.

The Cry of Courage

In answer to that call to courage, based upon the certainty of the Divine power and activity, there follows a great cry of courage expressed in three ways as the result of an upward look, a backward look, and a look into the future.

The upward look is fixed upon Jehovah; and the strength of His arm, as revealed in the victories won in ancient times, being remembered, the cry ascends, " Awake, awake, put on strength, O arm of the Lord."

The backward look rests upon that mighty deliverance wrought for the people when they were delivered from the bondage of Egypt by the way of the divided sea; and finds expression in the declaration that the victory there was won by this same arm of the Lord.

The onward look, out of such conviction of the present resource and of past triumph, is one of assurance; and expresses itself in the declaration of the certainty of the return of the ransomed to Zion, and the ending of all the circumstances of darkness and of desolation.

The Cause of Courage

Whereas the call to courage, and the cry of courage, have been evidently the result of the vision of Jehovah, and the assurance of His faithfulness; the underlying cause is finally

declared as in the words of Jehovah Himself.
All that the prophet has said to the people,
and in the name of the people in the spirit
of courage, is said in answer by Jehovah Himself; and the answer is to an upward look, a
look around, and an onward look.

As in their weakness they look up, Jehovah
answers by the declaration, " I, even I, am
He that comforteth you," and proceeds to rebuke them for any fear of man that may tarry
in their heart, declaring that such fear is the
outcome of forgetfulness of Him, Jehovah,
their Maker.

Looking around, the exile is seen in captivity, oppressed, and passing to death; but
the declaration of Jehovah is that of His presence and power, even in the midst of the
tempestuous sea.

The final word of Jehovah is addressed particularly to His Servant, and declares that
which had been already affirmed, that He has
put His words in His mouth, and covered Him
in the shadow of His hand, in order that He
may ultimately restore both the heavens and
the earth, and be able to say unto Zion, " Thou
art My people."

Thus these messages are all calculated to
create courage. In the cry to courage they
are challenged to look back to Abraham, to

look on to the nearness of God's activity, to look round without fear in the presence of opposition. Their cry of courage is due to the fact that they first look up to the arm of the Lord, and then look back and remember how He has delivered, and finally and consequently look on in the assurance that He will deliver. The declaration of the cause of courage is full of comfort as fear is rebuked as being due to forgetfulness of Jehovah, and Jehovah is pledged by His might to succour and establish His people.

γ. *Messages to the Afflicted*

The messages to the afflicted are of course to the same persons, but have to do principally with the fact of their affliction, setting it in the light of those certainties of deliverance which have been emphasized in the previous messages. The first affirms the end of suffering; the second describes the beginning of strength; while the third announces the return of Jehovah to His people.

The End of Suffering

The first message is one in which Jerusalem is called upon to awake because the end of her suffering is approaching. It is in some sense an answer to her cry, " Awake, awake, put on strength, O arm of the Lord." That was the cry of confidence; this is the answer of grace. The declaration is made that she has drunk and drained the cup of her sorrows.

This declaration is immediately followed by a graphic picture of her suffering. She has been bereft of her children, so that none of them have been able to take her by the hand and lead her. Overtaken by desolation and destruction, there has been none to bemoan her, and none to comfort her. Her sons have fainted and failed because of the judgments of God.

This cup of her affliction and suffering is to be taken out of her hand and put into the hand of such as have afflicted her.

The Beginning of Strength

The second message calls upon Zion to awake and put on her strength and her beautiful garments, in view of the fact that she is to be cleansed from all internal defilement. It is a further answer to the cry of courage in the midst of the messages of the faithful, " Awake, awake, put on strength, O arm of the Lord." As we have seen, that cry has been

answered in grace; and now it is answered in
such a way as to show the responsibility rest-
ing upon Zion.   While she is to be delivered
by the interference and action of Jehovah, she
is herself to resume her true position, shaking
herself from the dust, loosing herself from
bonds.

Though she had been sold into slavery for
naught, her redemption is determined on by
her God, Who already had delivered her from
Egypt and from Assyrian oppression, and
Who in the presence of the present oppression,
is still active.

By this deliverance she is to know the name
of Jehovah as that of the One Who is able
to accomplish His purpose.

The Return of Jehovah

The third message to the afflicted describes
the return of Jehovah to His people.   The fact
of this return is announced by runners and
watchmen, the burden of their good tidings being the re-affirmation of the abiding truth expressed in the word, " Thy God reigneth."

The return of Jehovah to Zion brings restoration and blessing, and results in an outburst
of song.   The waste places sing together in
celebration of the deliverance.   The cry of

courage asked for the awaking of the arm of
Jehovah, and for its clothing with strength.
The song celebrates the answer, " Jehovah hath
made bare His holy arm in the eyes of all
the nations."

The final movement of this message based
upon the certainty of the return of Jehovah is
that of a call to the people to cleanse themselves by separation from all unclean things,
and ends with the announcement that Jehovah
will go before the people, leading and guiding
them, and the God of Israel will be their rear-
ward, protecting them from all their enemies.

3. *The Completion of Suffering*

This final movement of the section which presents the Prince of peace as sustained through suffering, gives the profoundest unveiling, in the Scriptures of the Old Testament, of that suffering whereby the perfect Servant of God accomplishes His will, and thus makes possible the restoration of the sinning people, and the ransom and redemption of all peoples.

Here the value is most evidently Messianic. It is impossible to think of these words as fulfilled in the experience of Isaiah, Jeremiah, or any other than Jesus of Nazareth. There is a sense in which the principles revealed were expressed and exemplified in these great prophets of the past. Devoted to the will of God, and heroically proclaiming His word in the midst of a rebellious people, they were misunderstood and suffered accordingly; but in no sense were their sufferings vicarious. No healing for the wounds of their people resulted from their wounding. The prophet's own personal experiences are revealed here in a measure, but they are merged and almost lost sight of in the larger experiences of the perfect Servant Whom he describes. It is of great value that we notice the connection between the opening words here, " Behold, My Servant shall deal wisely," and the closing words of the section dealing with the consecration of the Servant to suffering, " Behold, the Lord will help Me." In that central section dealing with the suffering ministry, as we intimated in considering it, the prophet's own experiences were more patent. Now he proceeds to describe the actual sufferings of the Servant of God, Whose consecration to the pathway of suffering he had announced.

This movement falls into three parts. The first describes the ultimate triumph; the second deals with the pathway of suffering; and the third again, and in greater detail, declares the ultimate triumph.

This story of the profoundest sorrows of the Prince of peace is placed between declarations of His triumph through His sorrows.

α. The Ultimate Triumph

Of that Servant, Who in perfect abandonment to the will of God, and in absolute confidence in His sustaining power can say, " Behold, the Lord God will help Me "; the Lord is able to say, " Behold, My Servant shall deal wisely, He shall be exalted and lifted up, and shall be very high."

This lifting up and exaltation is of a two-fold nature. It is first the elevation of conspicuous sorrows. This is seen in the reason assigned for the astonishment of the people. "His visage was so marred more than any man, and His form more than the sons of men." It is also the elevation of conspicuous success, as the final words declare, "So shall He sprinkle many nations; kings shall shut their mouths at Him."

Two little words, "as" and "so," give this key of interpretation. It is by the way of sorrow that success is realized. "As many were astonied . . . so shall He sprinkle many." The astonishment was caused by the marred visage and form. By that suffering which astonished, He startles the nations and silences the kings. Thus the first movement of the prophetic word in setting forth the completion of the suffering of the Prince of peace, is an announcement of the ultimate triumph, and the revelation that this triumph will be the result of a process of pain, which will astonish the world.

β. The Pathway of Suffering

In this paragraph we reach the infinite depths, and analysis seems almost irreverent.

There is however, a very clearly defined movement, and we may trace it in all reverence.
The prophet described first the rejected ministry; secondly, the vicarious suffering; and
finally the atoning death of the Servant of
Jehovah, Who is the Prince of peace.

The Rejected Ministry

The first paragraph describes a rejected
ministry. If the opening words expressed the
experience either of Isaiah or Jeremiah or a
prophet of Israel in some other day, it is
noticeable that the writer almost immediately
diverted attention from himself, by speaking
or writing in the third person, as of another;
and this method is maintained to the end of
the section. The ministry described is that of
One Who was entirely misunderstood; " a tender plant " before Jehovah, a root full of the
potentialities of all loveliness, and this " out
of a dry ground "; that is, out of circumstances which had never produced anything of
excellence; yet to the eyes of those who saw
Him, without form or comeliness, and devoid
of beauty.

Therefore " He was despised and rejected
of men "; and consequently in His own experience, " a Man of sorrows, and acquainted

with grief"; and therefore again, still more
emphatically, One from Whom men hid their
faces, because they held Him in no estimation.
This is a prophetic picture of the Prince of
peace in the midst of the circumstances of
desolation, walking misunderstood on the low-
est plane of the degradation resulting from
sin, though Himself the perfect Servant, dealing wisely. It is the picture of the suffering
of a ministry of light in the midst of darkness, and the growing intensity of that suffering is remarkably set forth. Full of beauty
in the eyes of God, but without beauty which
men desire; therefore by them despised. The
result of this attitude filled His heart with
sorrows, the evidences of which were discover-
able in the marred visage. This made no appeal to men other than that of making them
turn their faces from Him, while they held
Him in no estimation.

The Vicarious Suffering

The prophetic word immediately proceeds
to an explanation of the real nature and value
of the suffering of the Servant of God. It
was vicarious suffering. He was suffering
not only with them, but for them; bearing
their griefs, carrying their sorrows. The ap-

palling degradation of man is revealed in the
fact that these sorrows were looked upon as
Divine judgments upon the Sufferer. "We
did esteem Him stricken, smitten of God, and
afflicted."

With an abrupt "But," the prophet cor-
rects the false view, and in clear and stately
language tells the truth about the suffering
of the perfect One. This statement needs no
exposition. "He was wounded for our transgressions, He was bruised for our iniquities;
the chastisement of our peace was upon Him;
and with His stripes we are healed."

The whole truth, both as to human sin, and
the method of the Divine grace, is finally
summarized in the declaration, "All we like
sheep have gone astray; we have turned every
one to his own way; and the Lord hath laid
on Him the iniquity of us all."

The Atoning Death

Finally the uttermost of suffering is reached
in the death of the Sufferer. To this death
He gave Himself in that awe-inspiring strength
of devotion which found its expression in dig-
nified silence.

So far as man was concerned, His death
was the ultimate in human oppression. Men

cared nothing that He was cut off out of the land of the living, and they gave Him burial with the wicked.

The inner meaning of the death is revealed in the words that flame with the light of infinite grace in the midst of the passage, " For the transgression of My people was He stricken."

γ. *The Ultimate Triumph*

Again the ultimate triumph is declared; and again, and with more of detail, it is set in relation to suffering.

The first movement declares that the pathway of pain leads to prosperity. There was a sense in which Jehovah put Him to grief, but it was in a holy and loving co-operation which had nothing in it of conflict, as between His Servant and Himself. By the way of the bruising, the grief, and the offering of His soul, the Servant passes to the triumph of the new race, and the endless life, and the victories of Jehovah.

The figure changes, and the same truth is repeated as the prophet shows that through the travail of the Servant the triumph is won. The newborn race of justified ones, springs from the travail and the birth-pangs of His unfathomable sorrows.

The whole movement ends where it began.
The beginning spoke of an exaltation of conspicuous sorrow, and of conspicuous success.
The final note is that of a glorious exaltation
resulting from a pouring out of life in a
death in which sins were borne, and sinners
prayed for.

Again let it be said that to suggest that
these words had fulfilment in any other than
the Christ of the New Testament is to reveal
an ignorance of their height and depth and
length and breadth of meaning, only equalled
by the blindness of those who saw no beauty
in Him that they should desire Him, and who
therefore saw nothing over which to grieve
in His sorrows and in His death.   It is a remarkable fact, not lightly to be ignored, that
every writer of the New Testament with the
exception of James and Jude, makes reference
to this particular paragraph, and links it to
the story of Christ.

ii. SINGING IN TRIUMPH

We now come to the second section in the division which presents the Prince of peace. It deals with the triumphant singing resulting from the completion of the work of the suffering Servant of God; and it consists of three clearly defined movements; first, the song of assurance; secondly, the prophet's consequent appeal; and finally, a description of the administration following the victory.

a. THE SONG OF ASSURANCE

This song sets forth the glorious fact of the restoration resulting from suffering; celebrating it first as to its grace, and secondly as to its glory.

1. *The Grace of Restoration*

In language full of exalted enthusiasm the song describes the blessings resulting to the people of God from the accomplishment by His Servant of His purpose through suffering and death. There is an almost startling abruptness in the first word, " Sing," as it follows the final declaration of the previous paragraph, " He poured out His soul unto death, and was numbered with the transgressors: yet He bare the sin of many, and made intercession for the transgressors." Out of that unfathomable sorrow there emerges the song which celebrates restoration. The intimate connection between the sorrows of the Servant, and the song of the ransomed must not be lost sight of. The whole emphasis in the first movement of the song is on the exceeding grace which makes such a song possible. The effects are traced to their original cause.

The first movement is one of rejoicing over the enlargement of the people. The barren and the destitute become fruitful and prosperous, and this so abundantly that it is necessary to enlarge the tent, and to lengthen the cords. The children of the restored nation are seen spreading through all lands, possessing the nations, and carrying with them the blessings of prosperity as they make the desolate cities to be inhabited.

The second movement reveals the cause of this prosperity. The widowed and desolate nation is restored and comforted. In an earlier part of the prophecy, Zion had been represented as complaining "Jehovah hath forsaken me; and the Lord hath forgotten me." This complaint was answered by the challenge of Jehovah, "Where is the bill of your mother's divorcement, wherewith I have put her away? or, which of my creditors is it to whom I have sold you? " That figure is now taken up, and the song declares that Jehovah of hosts is Husband and Redeemer of Zion; and that restoration to His favour and fellowship is the secret of the prosperity manifested in the increase of children, and enlargement of the borders.

Finally the forsaken and troubled wife is described as pardoned and at peace. The forsaking was only for a moment, and was necessary in order to the restoration. The kindness of Jehovah is everlasting, and His covenant of peace with His people will abide.

Thus the effect of restoration is traced to the activities of His grace, the movement being from the outward manifestations to the eternal sources in the heart of God.

The order of experience is that first of His mercy, resulting in a covenant of peace; and this must be explained by all that has gone before with reference to the suffering of His Servant. Growing out of that covenant, the nation is restored to a fellowship with Him, which is described under the figure of the marriage relationship, and as a fellowship that results in fruitfulness. The ultimate issue and experience is that which the song first celebrates, of a great and gracious prosperity, and the enlargement of all life.

2. *The Glory of Restoration*

The song continuing, now celebrates the glory issuing from grace, the whole emphasis in this second part being upon the glory. Here again the description proceeds from the material effect through the moral rectitude which preceded it, to the might of Jehovah which was at once the originating cause, and the abiding safeguard of the blessings. Zion is still addressed as in the midst of trouble, " afflicted, tossed with tempest, and not comforted," and in figurative language glowing with colour, and flaming with light, her material magnificence is described. She is seen as a city full of glory and of beauty, a city of strength and of safety, her stones, her foundations, her pinnacles, and her gates all radiant. All is suggestive of final and abiding stability in that she is built and beautified by the most precious things of earth.

Passing from the description of the things of external magnificence, the song reaches a higher level as it describes the moral rectitude of the people, which is the true cause of the splendour of the outward conditions. Beginning where all moral and spiritual values must begin, with the children, the song declares that they shall all be disciples of Jehovah, and consequently their peace shall be great. The civic strength shall be that of righteousness, and therefore from this city of God, all oppression will be banished, and fear and terror will be unknown. This is a perfect description of civic life at its highest. Children who are disciples of Jehovah, grow into a manhood which insists upon righteousness, and is intolerant only of oppression. Where these conditions obtain, the city must be one full of peace, and free from fear.

Finally the city thus established, and the people thus restored to true relationship with God, and consequent true inter-relationships, are impregnable. Enemies may gather together against such a city, but their coming will not be by the will of God, and consequently they will fail. There have been a smith and a weapon which have destroyed, which have been the creation of Jehovah; the inference of the statement being that this exercise of judgment has been due to the failure of the people morally. Where there is the fulfilment of the ideal, no enemy will be able to gain any advantage over the city, and no weapon formed against her can prosper. The final statement of the song, " This is the heritage of the servants of the Lord, and their righteousness which is of Me, saith Jehovah," repeats the truth perpetually taught throughout this second part of the prophecy, that the way of restoration is that of the Divine activity, and that the righteousness which ensures the strength and safety of the people is provided by Jehovah.　When the fall of Babylon was declared, and the promise was made, " I place salvation in Zion," the declaration was made, " I bring near My righteousness . . . and My salvation shall not tarry."　Since that declaration of the purpose of peace, the Prince of peace has been seen, traversing the pathway of His sorrows, and triumphing over sin therein; so that now the last note of the song of restoration declares " their righteousness is of Me, saith Jehovah."

b. THE GREAT APPEAL

Immediately following the song, we have the prophet's appeal. It is an appeal made in the consciousness of the victory won by the Servant of Jehovah, and the consequent possibility of restoration offered to the people. While the message is continuous, there are two special emphases. It first recognizes the need, and utters an appeal; and then utters an appeal on the basis of the consciousness of resource.

1. *The Need and the Appeal*

The need is inferred in the opening invitations. The message addresses those who are thirsty, hungry, and who are without money; and does so by declaring to them that there is perfect provision for all their need; water and bread, wine and milk.

That the description is not of material things but of spiritual, is evidenced by the fact that whereas the people are described as without money, it is nevertheless declared that they are spending money for that which is not bread. The message is to a people who have turned their back upon their own spiritual birthright, who are attempting to satisfy themselves with the things of the dust, and who are proving that the money they possess is not current in the realm whence the true water of life, and the bread of the spirit, are to be obtained.

The argument declares the unutterable folly of their attitudes and activities, in that they are spending " money for that which is not bread," and their " earnings for that which satisfieth not." The corrective for all this false activity on the part of the people is that they should hearken, and so find the true sustenance of life.

To these people the appeal is that they should give attention, and Jehovah promises that He will make an everlasting covenant with them. This covenant is the result of the work of the Servant of God Who is given for a Witness to the peoples, and as a Prince and Commander. The result of obedience, and of the consequent covenant, will be the fulfilment of the original purpose of God for His people; they will become the centre of attraction and blessing to nations beyond the covenant.

2. *The Appeal and the Resource*

All that which has been said leads up to, and is consummated in the central appeal.

This appeal is first uttered in general terms, and then in particular detail.

The general appeal recognizes the attitude of the Divine grace. While the people are thirsty and hungry and poverty-stricken in all spiritual matters, Jehovah is yet near, and may be found. Their responsibility is that they seek and call upon Him. While they are conscious of feverish unrest and dissatisfaction, all they need is at their disposal in the One against Whom they have sinned, and upon Whom they have turned their back. There can however be no appropriation of supply save by definite action on their part. They must seek, they must call upon God.

The particular appeal is characterized by the most remarkable clearness and simplicity of statement. So much is this so that even in the fuller light of the Christian revelation it abides as a clear and remarkable statement of the way of human salvation. It first indicates human responsibility, and so explains how men may seek and call upon the Lord in the words, " Let the wicked forsake his way, and the unrighteous man his thoughts: and let him return unto the Lord." It then utters the Divine promise, and supremely demonstrates the attitude of God in grace, " He will have mercy upon him . . . He will

abundantly pardon." So important is this
that it is well for us to consider it with care.
Human responsibility is stated first as to the
manifest attitude, " Let the wicked forsake
his way "; then as to the activity of the mind,
which must precede, " the unrighteous man
his thoughts "; and finally as to the inclusive
fact, which is at once the inspiration and accomplishment, " let him return unto the Lord."
Every way of wickedness is due to rebellion
against God. Therefore return to God is in
itself a thought of righteousness, and issues
in righteous conceptions; which, in turn, produce ways in harmony with the Divine purpose.

Yet by such obedience, man is not restored.
It is the condition of restoration. Restora-
tion is an act of the Divine grace, an act of
God. He it is Who in mercy pardons.

All this must also be interpreted in the
light of the revelation of the Servant of God,
Who through suffering makes possible this
attitude of Divine grace. The announcement
that God will have mercy, and will pardon,
is the result of all the process described in
the fifty-third chapter.

The prophet then proceeded to his argument
with the people in favour of such return to
God on their part; and the argument must

be taken in close connection with the declarations as to human responsibility and Divine promise, already made. The wicked is to forsake his way, and the unrighteous man his thought; and that because the thoughts of God are not the thoughts of the unrighteous, neither are the ways of the wicked the ways of God. This difference in thought has resulted in the difference in the way; and man's only restoration to blessing is that of turning from his own thought and way, in order to accept the thought and the way of Jehovah.

He then clearly declared what the difference is between the Divine and human thought and way, in the words, " For as the heavens are higher than the earth, so are My ways higher than your ways, and My thoughts than your thoughts." The thoughts of God for man include the heavens and all eternal things. The thoughts of man for himself have excluded the heavens; and he has attempted to discover satisfaction in the things which are only of the earth. The result has been that the ways of man have been ways of the earth, while the ways of God for man would have included all the facts and the forces of the heavens.

From this false conception and conduct of human life, a man is called to return to the

Lord, and to accept His thoughts, and to walk
in His ways.

Finally the prophet declared the resources
which are at the disposal of man as he returns.
These may be summarized as a perfect law,
and a perfect life.

The perfect law is first described under the
figure of rain and snow, which falling from
the heaven, do not return, but produce the
results of fruitfulness in the earth. Thus the
distinction between heaven and earth, as in-
dicating the difference between the Divine and
human conceptions, is maintained. In order
to satisfaction in the earth, it is necessary that
there should be this gift from the heavens.
Passing from the figure to the actual fact,
the prophet declares that as are the rain and
snow to the earth, so is the Word of God to
the life of man. Man attempting to satisfy
himself with the earth, fails. Man living in
the law of God, thinking according to the
Word of God, which is the revelation of the
will of God; finds the secret of his own life
as he realizes the purposes of God.

The appeal ends with a description of that
perfect life which results from obedience to
the Word of God, which is full of poetic
beauty and suggestiveness. Such life is to
be one of liberty and joy. In the power of

it, men go out with joy, and are led forth with peace. The figure is that of escape from all bondage and all limitation into the spaciousness of a great liberty. The joy is to be that of the true apprehension of the things of the earth; or perhaps it would be more correct to say that it is the joy of bringing the things of the earth to their fulfilment. Mountains and hills break forth into singing before the people who are living according to the law of Jehovah. The trees of the field break out into glad applause under the influence of these people. The presence of redeemed humanity issues in the redemption of Nature. Instead of the thorn, there comes up the fir-tree; instead of the brier, there springs the myrtle-tree. The sons of God in the power of His life, and according to His law, bring to the whole creation the forces and healing of renewal.

Everything reaches its finality in the glorifying of Jehovah. This declaration not only reveals the fact that this is the ultimate purpose of human life, but also that Jehovah is only satisfied and glorified when human life comes to its fulness of realization.

c. THE ADMINISTRATION

This division dealing with the Prince of peace closes with a section setting forth certain aspects of the administration of the kingdom, which may thus be summarized: the welcome to strangers; the judgment of evil; the restoration of the contrite; and the final word.

1. *The Welcome to Strangers*

The message of welcome to the strangers is intended for the comfort of those who by reason of the promises of restoration made to the people of God are likely to be discouraged. The stranger will probably say, " The Lord will surely separate me from His people "; and the eunuch, in view of the hope of the growth of the nation, may declare, " Behold, I am a dry tree." Both of these are comforted.

The message of comfort to them is introduced by a call to the chosen people, in which their responsibility is declared in the charge that they keep judgment, and do righteousness. These are the things in which they have signally failed, and therefore the prophet now reminded them of the resources at their disposal for obedience. Jehovah declares, " My

salvation is near to come, and My righteousness to be revealed "; and here, as constantly
through this whole movement, we must in-
terpret the meaning of the affirmation by the
revelation of the Prince of peace, Who, as
Servant of God, brings salvation and righteousness near.   By fulfilment of this responsibility, in the strength of this resource, the
people come to the realization of blessing.
There is a balance between the renewed statement of conditions upon which blessing is
realized, and the first charge.   That charge
was to keep judgment and do righteousness.
The condition of blessing is that the man shall
do this, that is, righteousness; and the son
of man hold fast by it, that is, by judgment.
Two illustrations are given; the first that
which has been through all the history of the
people of God the sign of complete sanctifica-
tion to His will, the keeping of the Sabbath;
and the second that of the conduct which
harmonizes therewith, the keeping of the hand
from the doing of evil.

Into these covenants of responsibility and
of blessing the stranger is admitted.   The
probable laments are forbidden, and the promises of Jehovah are uttered.   To the eunuchs
the promise is made of a memorial, and a name
in the house of God, better than that of sons

and daughters; but the blessing to them is carefully conditioned upon their observance of responsibility. They also are to keep the Sabbaths, and choose the things that please God, and hold fast by His covenant. To these childless men, such obedience will result in a name that shall not be cut off.

Identical responsibilities are laid upon the strangers. The conditions upon which they are received are that they join themselves to the Lord to serve Him, to love His name. They also must keep the Sabbath and hold fast by the covenant. These responsibilities being fulfilled, they are welcomed to the holy mountain, and to all the joy of the house of prayer. Their offerings and sacrifices are acceptable, and that because the house of the Lord is a house of prayer for all peoples.

The final word reveals the prophet's understanding of the fact that in the administration of the kingdom there will be a wider application than that to the chosen people. Jehovah will gather the outcasts of Israel, but He will also gather others, who, in association with His own, will enter into all the blessings of covenant relationship.

2. *The Judgment of Evil*

While there is welcome for all who submit to the Lord, there is to be the severest judgment of evil, even when manifested among the chosen people. To the declaration of that judgment the prophet next turned, dealing first with the spiritual leaders; and secondly, with the apostate people.

α. *The spiritual Leaders*

In an abrupt and almost startling transition the prophetic word changes from the tone of comfort to that of severity. The beasts of the field and the beasts of the forest are summoned to devour. If the marginal reading here, which suggests that this summons is one addressed to the beasts of the field to devour the beasts of the forest be adopted, then the beasts of the forest are the false shepherds, through whose failure the flock has suffered. No material difference is made in the real teaching of the message; for if the suggestion of the text be followed, that both beasts of the field and beasts of the forest are called to devour, then those to be devoured are not the sheep of the flock, but the dumb dogs, who cannot bark. This opening cry to the beasts,

brief and forceful, is the announcement of
judgment upon the false spiritual leaders.

The reason of this judgment is then declared
in detail, and with tremendous force. It is
first that of the pollution of the leader. The
prophet declared that they are ignorant;—
blind, without knowledge, dumb dogs, unable
to bark; that they are indolent;—dreaming,
lying down, loving to slumber. This double
charge reveals their failure to fulfil their true
shepherd function. He then showed that that
failure is due to what they are in themselves,
as he described them as being greedy; unable
to understand, they are seeking their own way,
and their own gain; moreover, they are sensual; loving wine, and turning the days into
opportunities for carousal.

The result of this is then set forth. It is
that of the suffering of the godly, and the
indifference of the godless to that suffering.
This is always the effect produced when the
spiritual leaders of a people become sensual
and selfish. Those who under such rule walk
in uprightness, find no resting-place other
than death and the grave. The men who are
the true strength of a people perish, and pass
away; and because their value is not understood, their perishing is not mourned.

β. *The apostate People*

Still dealing with the judgment of evil, the prophet declared that the people who yield to the evil influences of their leaders are also to be judged. These are summoned to hear their own denunciation. Their sin has been exalted and manifest, and their judgment is to be conspicuous and complete; and with these things the prophet dealt particularly.

The terms of the summons at once reveal the prophet's estimate of the heinousness of the sin of the people. He described them as " sons of the sorceress," and as " the seed of the adulterer and the whore "; which descriptions significantly emphasized the prophet's conceptions of the supremacy of spiritual relationships. He was speaking undoubtedly to those who after the flesh are of the chosen people; but because they have followed in the sins of idolatry and unfaithfulness to the great covenant with Jehovah, which had been the sins of their fathers, they are thus described. The suggestiveness of this description is the more remarkable in the light of the first movement in this description of administration, in which the prophet had declared that strangers, that is, those not the actual seed according to the flesh, are admitted to all

the benefits of the covenant upon the fulfilment of conditions; while here he described
the actual children according to the flesh, by
terms which put them outside all the benefits
because of their continuity in the sins of idolatry and unfaithfulness.

His charge against them is threefold.

Their attitude is that of insolence as is
revealed by the questions which he asked.
They sport themselves against Jehovah, they
make a wide mouth, and draw out the tongue.

This description of the attitude of insolence
merges into the charge of idolatry, which vin-
dicates his description of them as "the seed
of the adulterer and the whore"; and that
this was the intention of the prophet is seen
in the fact that he said, "Are ye not children,
a seed of falsehood?" as he commenced to describe the idolatries. These idolatries, as we
have seen, have been exalted and manifest.
They have been indulged in the valleys; the
chosen people have descended to the most de-
grading rites of heathen superstition in that
they have sacrificed their children. To the
smooth ones, that is, the deceitful ones, the
deceitful gods of the valleys, they have made
their offerings. Their idolatries moreover
have been upon the high and lofty mountain.
They have invaded the sanctity of the house-

hold, which sin the prophet described as peculiarly that of spiritual harlotry, of unfaithfulness to the covenant with Jehovah, the supreme symbol of which He had made that of the marriage relation. Even their policies had been affected by harlotry, in that when dealing with kings through their ambassadors, they had debased themselves to this underworld of evil.

Finally their sin had been that of their complete and overwhelming infatuation. Wearied with the length of the way, they had nevertheless been persistent therein; and that because they had been enslaved by a false fear, the outcome of the fact that they had forgotten God.

For these reasons judgment must fall upon the apostate people in the hour of the administration of the kingdom. The judgment will take the form, first of exposure. Jehovah will declare the righteousness of the people, that is, will show its hollowness and reveal the fact of the profitlessness of all idolatry. Upon such sin, vengeance must fall, and when it comes, the rabble of the idols in which the people have put their trust, will be unable to deliver, for the wind of the Divine wrath will sweep them away.

In this judgment however there will be

discrimination, for he who trusts in Jehovah will possess the land and inherit the holy mountain; and such a remnant will create a highway, along which Jehovah will travel for the establishment of the Kingdom, as in co-operation with Him, they prepare the way, and remove the stumbling-blocks.

3. *The Restoration of the Contrite*

Yet again the declaration of administration turns to such as are contrite and penitent. There is no break in the message, for those referred to in the closing sentences of the paragraph dealing with the judgment of evil, are now described in greater detail, and their relationship to Jehovah is declared.

α. The Speaker

This passage is full of beauty, first as it describes the Speaker, Jehovah. His essential glories are named in brief sentences, full of dignity, and of beauty.

He is " the High and lofty One." This is peculiarly Isaiah's vision of God. It was this vision of the Lord sitting upon a throne high and lifted up, which had called him to a higher plane of prophesying. It is the vision of One Whose supremacy is established, and whose government is victorious.

He is the One " that inhabiteth eternity." This word translated " eternity " really suggests ultimate duration in the sense of perpetuity. Its significance is that of being without beginning and without end. It is the ever-present now. Man thinks and speaks in terms of his own limitation, of the then, of the where; but in everywhen and in everywhere Jehovah is. It is one of the sublimest words of the Old Testament in its revelation of all that we now mean by eternity. To whatever limit our imagination can carry us, of time or of space, we find God. Again the thought is that of Isaiah, who in the great vision of the coming One in the earlier movements of the book, described Him as "the Father of eternity."

His "name is Holy." This is a declaration of the character of God, the root signification of the word being that of purity.

Having thus described the essential glories of Jehovah, the prophet then referred to the activities of His grace. These activities proceed from two bases of operation. God dwells in the high and holy place, and also with him that is of a contrite and humble spirit. Into such a spirit He brings all the forces and resources of His own abiding place. Into that abiding place of holiness He brings all the need of the contrite and humble spirit.

The purposes for which He thus dwells in the high and holy place, and with him of contrite and humble spirit, are those of revival, that is, of renewal of life.

All this is an unveiling of the glory and the

grace of Jehovah, and prepares the way for the great proclamation which immediately follows.

β. The Proclamation

The first word of the proclamation is one which declares the limitation of wrath. Jehovah announces that He will not contend for ever, neither will He be always wroth, for if He did, those with whom He dealt would faint away, and be destroyed.

The reason of the wrath had been that of the sin, and the persistence therein, of His people.

Now he will proceed with the activity of grace. This is declared by a statement, " I have seen his ways, and will heal him," which most evidently refers to the condition of the contrite and humble spirit which had already been described. These ways are responded to by healing, leading, and restoration.

The whole value of the mission of the Prince of peace is declared in the great words, " Peace, peace, to him that is far off and to him that is near, saith Jehovah; and I will heal him."

4. The Final Word

This section of the division revealing the Prince of peace ends with the same solemn affirmation with which the first division, dealing with the purpose of peace, ended; that there is no peace to the wicked.

Here it is even more emphatic, in that it is preceded by a declaration of the restlessness of the wicked. They are like the troubled sea which cannot rest.

Thus while in the great economy of God He gives to men the Prince of peace, His people were again solemnly warned that there could be no appropriation of the benefits of His ministry while they persisted in wickedness.

The picture presented to the mind by this second division is still that of the chosen people of God in the midst of circumstances of danger and difficulty almost amounting to desolation. The prophetic note is however, even more emphatically one of comfort as it presents the Servant of God, seen in the first division, in clearer outline and fuller detail. In Him the majesty and might and mercy of Jehovah, revealed in the first division, are seen merging into operation, which through suffering leads on to triumph. The next division, depending upon all that has been revealed of the purpose of peace, and of the Prince of peace, describes the programme of peace.

III. THE PROGRAMME OF PEACE

We now commence the last section of the prophecies of peace, which deals with the programme of peace. There are three distinct movements, dealing in turn with the declarations of conditions; the ultimate realization; and the principle of discrimination; the prophet ending all with a final word of application.

i. THE DECLARATIONS OF CONDITIONS

The burden of this part of the prophecy is its insistence upon the necessity for morality according to the Divine conception. Whereas the purpose of Jehovah is peace, this purpose can only be realized on the basis of purity. While Jehovah through His Servant will bring near His righteousness and salvation, and accomplish the work; the work to be accomplished, in order to peace, is that of the realization of life according to the Divine intention. This subject is dealt with by the prophet in three ways. The moral requirements are declared; moral failure is confessed; and moral victory is won.

a. MORAL REQUIREMENTS DECLARED

The prophet revealed the moral requirements by a condemnation of formalism, and a description of true religion, thus emphasizing the fact that morality must be the expression of religion, and therefore that religion is only acceptable as it issues in morality.

1. *The Charge to the Prophet*

The first brief paragraph consists of the charge to the prophet. He is to declare to the people of God the fact of their sin, and he is to do it with courage, without uncertainty, and with insistence. In an understanding of their sin, they will be brought to a recognition of the conditions necessary for the establishment of peace.

2. *Formalism*

The chief sin of the people of God consisted in the degradation of religion by formalism, and therefore formalism is dealt with in a passage which is perhaps the most striking in the Bible as revealing how near mere formalism approaches in outward appearance to true religion, and at the same time what an impassable gulf yawns between them.

The observances of formalism are those of orthodox and regular ceremonial, accompanied by intellectual delight therein. They seek God daily. They are as diligent in the ordinance of God as though they did righteousness; and in this activity they take delight. Can anything more be needed?

Immediately following this description of the observances of formalism, the prophet utters the complaint which it is making. These formalists complain of the Divine blindness, and the Divine indifference as they inquire why it is that God does not see their fasting, and that He takes no knowledge when they afflict the soul. This complaint reveals the fact that something more is needed, that there is a lack; and it clearly shows that the lack, even in the consciousness of the formalists, is that of God. An intellectual delight in the knowledge of His ways, and in the activity of drawing near, is not answered by the spiritual satisfaction of a true fellowship. Why is this?

The inquiry of the formalists is answered, and in the answer we have a revelation of the iniquity of formalism. These people, regular in religious observance, and taking intellectual delight therein, are living in a threefold sin. Their fasting is merely for their

own pleasure, and while they fast, they are
sinning against their neighbours in that they
are oppressing their labourers.

While they fast they are sinning against
themselves, because they are occupied with
each other; and strife and contention and
smiting with the fist of wickedness is the result.   The purpose of their fasting is not that
their voice may be heard on high, even though
they complain that God is indifferent.

Finally the sin of formalism is that it is
a sin against Jehovah.   He has not chosen
such fasting.   He does not accept the outward
and external attitudes and activities of men
at worship, while they wrong their neighbours,
contend among themselves, and in the deepest
of their desire, are not seeking Him.

3. *True Religion*

From this unmasking of formalism the
prophet immediately turned to an unveiling
of true religion, and that in the three applica-
tions already suggested by the revelation of
the iniquity of formalism, those namely of
neighbours, self, and Jehovah.   In doing this
he shows in each case the duty and the reward.

True religion finds its expression towards
neighbours in setting them free from every

kind of bondage; and in the activities of caring for all those in need, the hungry, the poor, and the naked. Where that duty is fulfilled, light breaks forth as the morning, and the soul finds its healing, its strength, and its defence in Jehovah. Such religion brings the soul into that fellowship with Jehovah wherein His answer to the cry of the worshipper will be immediate, and the complaint of formalism be made impossible.

True religion finds its own self-expression in the activities already described. The true self-consciousness is that of compassion for the hungry, and desire to satisfy those who are afflicted. Where that is the condition of soul, light rises in darkness. There is the immediate consciousness of the guidance of Jehovah Who satisfies the soul, and the life is full of fruitfulness. Such life moreover, becomes influential in the restoration of waste places, and the reconstruction of a lost order.

True religion as to Jehovah, consists in delight in His will; and here once again the Sabbath is made the sacramental symbol of such delight. Where the soul delights in the will of Jehovah, its reward is that of delight in Jehovah Himself, which in turn issues in victorious and reigning life.

b. MORAL FAILURE CONFESSED

From that declaration of moral requirement, the prophet passed to the confession of moral failure; first by acknowledgment of the reason for national suffering, and then by definite confession.

1. *The Reason for National Suffering*

In dealing with formalism, the prophet had voiced the complaint of the formalists that God was blind and indifferent. Now he declared that the reason for the experiences of suffering, which made the people affirm of God this blindness and indifference, was not in Jehovah. " His hand is not shortened, that it cannot save; neither His ear heavy, that it cannot hear." All they suffered, as they had tacitly confessed, through the inactivity of Jehovah, must be accounted for in some other way. He is neither unable nor ignorant.

The real reason is then immediately declared. That which separated between them and God was the fact of their iniquities and their sins.

The declaration is followed by a terrible description of the sin of the people, first as to immoral conduct, and secondly as to the corrupt character out of which such conduct sprang.

The whole conduct of life is polluted. The hands, the fingers, the lips, the tongue are alike impure. In the affairs of human inter-relationship there is an absence of righteous-ness and truth, and the practice of deceit and lying.

All this results from a character which is utterly corrupt, and which the prophet de-scribes in a series of graphic statements, in which the relations between the underlying conceptions of life and the resulting conduct are set forth.

As to conception they hatch basilisks' eggs, and weave the spider's web; with the result that whoso eats of the eggs dies, or if one be crushed, it breaks out into a viper; the webs they weave are useless as garments, for they are works of iniquity, and acts of vio-lence. The activities of their feet tend to murder, because their thoughts are those of iniquity. Desolation and destruction are in their highways because they are ignorant of the way of peace. These are the causes of suffering, the reason why God neither hears nor answers.

2. *The Confession*

At once the prophet uttered the confession, "therefore is judgment far from us," and so on. He described the suffering anew. It is that of the darkness of which the formalists complained, that darkness which is the answer to their desire for light. It is a darkness which issues in confusion. Because of lack of light, guidance is sought as blind men seek it—from the wall. Even at noon-day there is stumbling, and all essential strength is absent. The issue of this darkness and confusion is lamentation.

Finally in definite words, the actual confession is made. It expresses itself first in the language of conviction. Transgressions, sins, iniquities are before God, and known by the people. Then in detail these things are confessed. The root of all the trouble has been that of denying Jehovah and turning away from following God. The fruit growing from such root has been that of oppression, and falsehood; so that judgment and righteousness and truth are violated, and the man who would depart from evil is made a prey.

This is the true story of the cause of all the suffering, and the confession is complete.

c. MORAL VICTORY WON

The last movement in the declarations of conditions sets forth the action of Jehovah whereby, in spite of all the failure, the moral victory is ultimately to be won. Its teaching stands out in clear relief in the forefront of the whole section; and the things already considered serve as background, throwing it up into brighter relief. It is a declaration of Jehovah's knowledge which the formalists have denied; of Jehovah's judgment in the presence of the lack of judgment amongst the failing people; and of Jehovah's Redeemer, appearing when the sinning people are unable to deliver themselves.

1. *Jehovah's Knowledge*

All that which has been confessed, Jehovah saw, and was displeased with.

He saw moreover, that there was no intercessor, that is, no one able to interfere as between the sinning people and Himself in such a way as to bring salvation and establish righteousness.

2. *Jehovah's Judgment*

In the presence of the conditions of sin and of helplessness which He thus knew, the action

of Jehovah was that of Himself becoming
what His people needed, in order to their
salvation, and the vindication of His righteousness. The presentation of this fact is one
which supremely emphasizes the loneliness of
Jehovah in this activity. It was activity by
His own strength, for " His own arm brought
salvation unto Him; His righteousness, it upheld Him."

His judgment was accomplished in His own
attributes. His coat of mail was righteousness, His helmet was salvation, His clothing
was vengeance, and His enveloping cloak was
zeal. These are all things of His own nature,
the attributes of His essence, which is Love.

His activity was for His own vindication a
manifestation of His unalterable justice. According to man's deeds He must act; and His
dealing with adversaries and enemies must be
in the nature of recompense.

The ultimate purpose of this activity is that
of His own glory, which glory is achieved
only as men fear His name.

3. *Jehovah's Redeemer*

The expression of that knowledge and that
judgment is finally the presentation of His
Redeemer. The prophet declared that He will

come to Zion, that is, to the abiding centre of that national life, the purpose of which was the glory of God in the blessing of the world. He will come moreover, to "them that turn from transgression in Jacob," that is to a remnant of faithful souls.

The result of His coming will be a new covenant of the Spirit and the Word to abide to perpetuity. This last declaration is addressed, by a transition of method, to the Redeemer Who comes to Zion; and the seed resulting from the advent of the Redeemer is that in which the Spirit and the Word are to abide for the accomplishment of the purpose of peace.

Thus the first condition for the carrying out of the programme of peace is that of a morality springing out of true religion. The condition upon which there may be a realization of such morality among a sinning and corrupt people, is that of their conviction of sin and confession thereof. Seeing that such conviction and confession cannot of themselves produce the fulfilment of the fundamental requirement, Jehovah becomes the Redeemer, and thus by His own activity brings the people to the fulfilment of the fundamental condition as He restores them to Himself.

ii. THE ULTIMATE REALIZATION

Having insisted upon the fulfilment of moral conditions as the fundamental necessity in the programme of peace, the prophecy becomes a glorious description of the ultimate realization of the purposes of God. This description deals first with material prosperity; then with spiritual realization; and finally with vocational fulfilment.

a. MATERIAL PROSPERITY

The description of material prosperity may be spoken of as a portrayal of the dawning of a new day, and its waxing to high noon. It falls into four parts; the daybreak; the returning exiles; the established city; and the glories of the perfect day.

1. *The Daybreak*

The central fact is that of light shining upon Zion. This must be taken in connection with the preceding section. Confession of sin has been made, and the activity of Jehovah as Redeemer has been declared. That is the light which is shining upon the people of God. The city is personified as one sitting amid

prevailing darkness, but herself illuminated
by the light and glory of Jehovah which shines
upon her. In view of this she is commanded
to arise and shine. The light that falls upon
her is not for her alone, but for those who
are in the darkness. The nations, seeing the
glory of the restored people of God, crowd
to the light. All this is the picture of the
first flush of dawn.

2. *The returning Exiles*

The illuminated and illuminating city is
commanded to lift the eyes, and look at the
gathering of the peoples. Among those who
come are her own sons and daughters, returning to the city long forsaken, but now re-
visited. Wealth of all kinds is poured into
her, and is accepted as an offering made upon
the altar of Jehovah, the first value of which
is that it beautifies the house of His glory.
The gathering of the peoples to the glorified
city is poetically described as the flight of
doves to the windows. Their gathering, accompanied by their wealth, is for the glory of
the name of Jehovah, and results from His
glorification of His people.

3. *The Established City*

Those who are thus gathered to the glory of the light become workers who build the walls. Their kings, not as slaves, but by the constraint of the grace of the illumination, serve the city. The fear of invasion and destruction has passed away, and the gates stand open continually for the reception of the wealth of the nations. Nations or kingdoms that oppose must perish. All the precious things of the land will contribute to the beautifying of the sanctuary of God. The sons of those who in bygone days had afflicted the people of God will come in willing submission, and confessing that Zion is indeed the city of Jehovah, the Holy One of Israel.

The city that has long sat solitary and desolate will become the centre of all the nations, and will learn experimentally the great truth so often declared by the prophets, that Jehovah is Saviour and Redeemer, the mighty One of Jacob.

4. *The high Noon*

The last phase is that of the ultimate prosperity. Gradually the light has overcome the darkness as day has advanced, and now the perfect realization of the purposes of God is described.

It is first that of perfect government. The multiplying of the material prosperity is described in a poetic figure as the transmutation of all the lower to the higher. Gold is to supersede brass; silver, iron; brass, wood; and iron, stones; and all this because under the supreme authority of Jehovah, government will be vested in rulers who produce peace by promoting righteousness. The issue of this will be that violence, desolation, and destruction, which have so long abounded, even in the city of God, will be for ever banished.

The result of perfect government will be perfect glory. The true light of the city will be neither sun by day, nor moon by night, but the presence of Jehovah, and the manifestation of His glory.

Because such irradiation is abiding, there will be no sunset, and no shadows; and perfect gladness will be the outcome of the abounding righteousness of the people, who will inhabit the land for ever. The last word of the description re-emphasizes the constantly repeated truth that all this will be the result of the work of Jehovah, Who will hasten it in His time.

While this is the picture of material pros-

perity, it is nevertheless the revelation of the
fact that such prosperity issues only from
moral rectitude; and the supreme impression
made upon the mind is that of the last note
of the former section, that the glorious result
is produced by the action of Jehovah Himself.
He it is Who rises in glory upon His people.

Nevertheless they are responsible in that
they are called upon to respond to the light
by arising and shining. As they do so, they
come into the place of abounding blessing,
and become the means of blessing to all those
upon whom their light shines. Thus the ultimate intention of God for His people, that
they shall be the means of blessing to others,
is never lost sight of.

b. SPIRITUAL REALIZATION

Passing from the description of material prosperity, the prophecy describes the inner secret, that namely of spiritual realization. This again falls into three parts; the first dealing with the anointed Messenger; the second with the priestly people; and the last consisting of the resulting song. The whole of this is really the language of the Servant of the Lord, Who is the Prince of peace, the One through Whom the purpose of peace is fulfilled.

1. *The anointed Messenger*

This first paragraph affords a new description of the Servant of the Lord as to His equipment, His mission, and His victory.

The fact of the equipment is declared in the brief but suggestive opening sentence, " The Spirit of the Lord God is upon Me." Of course this becomes most interesting in the light of the use made of this passage by Christ, Whose whole mission, from the mystery of His conception in the womb of the Virgin by the overshadowing of the Holy Spirit, to His death upon the Cross when He offered Himself through the eternal Spirit, was fulfilled in the power of the Spirit.

In the description of His mission the
prophecy first sets forth the first phase thereof,
that of the preaching of good tidings, binding
up the broken-hearted, the proclamation of
liberty to captives, and the setting free of the
prisoners. This is immediately followed by
a brief statement that takes in the whole mission of the Servant of God. Its first phase
is that of proclaiming the acceptable year of
the Lord. Its second is that of proclaiming
the day of vengeance of God. Its third is
that of comforting those who mourn. It is
impossible to read this without remembering
at what point Jesus ceased His reading in the
synagogue. He read the description of the
first phase to which we have already referred,
and the summarizing of it, ending with the
words, " to proclaim the acceptable year of the
Lord." The proclamation of the day of vengeance of God has not yet commenced, and
consequently that which is referred to by the
prophet as the comfort of all that mourn has
not yet commenced. The last movement in
this description of the mission deals with that
final phase, the comforting of those who
mourn. That will take place when Zion is
restored, and the ancient people of God fulfil
their true function of ministry in the world.

In the previous section dealing with ma-

terial prosperity, when describing the high
noon of prosperity, the prophet declared that
the people of God should be the branch of
His planting, the work of His hands, that He
might be glorified. That is now repeated in
this connection; for the restoration of Zion,
and of the people thereto, will be in order that
they might be trees of righteousness, the planting of the Lord, that He might be glorified.
Thus the ultimate victory of the Servant of
God will be that of this restoration, in which
the redeemed people shall take part, as they
build the old wastes, and make to cease the
desolations of many generations. In this
work the nations who are blessed by their
restoration will co-operate. Strangers will
feed their flocks, and aliens be their plowmen
and vine-dressers.

2. *The priestly People*

In that great future the people of God will
fulfil the true office of priesthood. When
Israel emerged from Egypt, the word of God
to them had been, " If ye will obey My voice
indeed, and keep My covenant, then ye shall
be a peculiar treasure unto Me from among
all peoples: for all the earth is Mine: and ye
shall be unto Me a kingdom of priests, and

an holy nation." This ideal has never yet
been perfectly fulfilled by the Hebrew people,
but it will be, as the result of the work of
the Servant of the Lord; and then men will
know them and name them as the ministers
of God.

In that day they will enter into true co-
operation with these nations, sharing their
wealth, and boasting in their glory. It will
be to them a day of compensation for all their
shame, and the nations will share in that
compensation. It is well to notice the change
here from the pronouns " ye," and " your " as
the people of God are addressed, to " they "
and " them " and " their," as the nations are
referred to.

The great new covenant with Israel is then
declared, and the Servant of God being still
the Speaker, speaks of Himself as " I, Jehovah." The foundation of the covenant is
laid in the righteousness of Jehovah in that
He loves judgment and hates robbery with
iniquity. The nature of the covenant is an
activity in truth, and therefore it is an everlasting one. The effect of it will be that His
people, redeemed from shame, will exert an
influence of righteousness among the peoples,
who in their turn will recognize the truth,
and submit themselves to it.

3. *The Song*

The message concerning spiritual realization ends with a song of praise, which is undoubtedly the song of the Servant of God, and therefore becomes also the song of the true Israel of God.

Jehovah is the fount of joy, and the reason of joy is first that of personal blessing. The Servant is clothed in salvation, and robed in righteousness by Jehovah; and therefore is seen acting in harmony with Jehovah, so that righteousness and praise spring forth before all the nations.

c. VOCATIONAL FULFILMENT

Having thus dealt with material prosperity, and with spiritual realization, the prophecy now describes in greater detail the vocational fulfilment. The new commencement indicates the fact that whether the message is part of the speech of the Servant of God, or that of the prophet himself, it is uttered in the midst of circumstances of incompleteness. The fulfilment is not yet, but it is certain. The description first deals with the restoration of the city as it speaks of the new names which she is to bear; secondly, it describes the watchmen, who look to the consummation; and finally affirms the certainty of the ultimate realization.

1. *The New Names*

The desire of the speaker is twofold. It is a passion for Zion, for Jerusalem; that there may be fulfilled in the experience of the city of God all the gracious promises which have been made; that her righteousness may go forth as brightness, and her salvation as a lamp that burneth. As we have seen in previous considerations, the city is to arise and shine because the light of the glory of Jehovah falls upon her. That is the consummation which is desired. The deeper passion is for that which will result from such spiritual prosperity. Thereby the nations will see the righteousness and the glory, and Jehovah will be vindicated.

There is no uncertainty in the heart of the speaker, and the notes of certainty are declared by the fourfold use of the words " Thou shalt." First the city is to be called by a new name, which the mouth of Jehovah shall name. Secondly it is to be filled with glory as it becomes a crown of beauty in the hand of Jehovah, and a royal diadem in the hand of God. Thirdly, the old names of the city and of the land are to pass away. The city has been termed Forsaken, and the land Desolate. Finally, the city is to be called Hephzibah, that is, My delight is in her; and the land Beulah, that is, married.

The reason of the certainty is the constantly affirmed fact that the Lord delights in the city, and therefore God will yet rejoice over her as the bridegroom rejoiceth over the bride.

2. *The Watchmen*

The certainty of ultimate fulfilment is made still more evident by this paragraph in which

the prophecy describes the watchmen on the
walls. These are the Lord's remembrancers,
and their occupation is that of ceaseless intercession with Him on behalf of Jerusalem, until
He make it a praise in the earth.

The answer to that intercession is then declared. It is the answer of Jehovah Who
swears by His right hand, and by the arm of
His strength, that He will accomplish all His
purposes, and that the city shall be restored
to prosperity. The oppression and spoiling
which have so long continued, will cease; and
the city will enter into all the prosperity of
her own labour, as the result of the action
of Jehovah.

3. *The Realization*

With vehement desire the messenger turns
to the people, charging them to prepare the
highway, declaring anew the fact of the coming of salvation in the coming of One Whose
reward is with Him. The result of this coming will be that of the restoration of the people
to holiness through redemption, and so to
influence.

A review of this section dealing with ultimate realization, will show the inter-relationship between those three facts, which consti-

tute its divisions. While material prosperity
is first dealt with, and the glory of the people
in the day of ultimate realization is made
perfectly clear, the central truth is that material prosperity can only result from spiritual
relationship. It is only when the people of
God realize the Divine ideal of priestly ministry that there can be the realization of material prosperity. Finally, the supreme value
of spiritual realization, and of material prosperity, is that of the fulfilment of vocation.
Not for her own sake is the city to be beautiful
and prosperous, but in order that she may be
a centre to which others may turn, to share in
her blessings; and the deepest note of all is
that of the glory of God, and the vindication
of His honour in the world. Yet it is impossible to consider this whole section without
coming to a new consciousness that the honour of God is vindicated, and that His name
is glorified, as blessing abounds, and men are
brought into realization of a perfect and abiding peace.

iii. THE PRINCIPLE OF DISCRIMINATION

This final section of the prophecy sets forth
anew the operation of the principle of discrimination in the methods of God. All the
blessing which has been described can only result from holiness; and ere that can be established, there must be a period of judgment.
At this point it is of supreme importance that
we recognize the connection between what we
are about to consider, and the declaration of
the anointed Messenger concerning His mission. In our study of that, we drew attention
to the fact that when Jesus cited the passage
in the synagogue, He ended with the words,
" to proclaim the acceptable year of the Lord."
The next phrase is, " the day of vengeance of
our God." That is the theme of this final section. In the order of actual happening, all
now to be described precedes the ultimate realization already considered. The prophet's
declaration concerning the moral conditions
which are necessary to restoration, and his
picture of the ultimate realization necessitate
this final teaching. How can there be perfect
restoration and fulfilment of vocation? The
answer to such an inquiry is contained in this
last section which describes the pathway of
judgment; records the prayer of desire; and

finally presents the operation of judgment in the sifting of the people.

a. THE PATHWAY OF JUDGMENT

This paragraph presents two pictures, that of the Warrior, and that of the conflict. It is important that we should at once note that the description is that of the Warrior returning from the conflict. While the conflict is described, it is from the standpoint of its completion.

1. *The Warrior*

The inquiry of the prophet reveals to us the vision which he saw. It was that of a Warrior coming from Edom, the word here being used as symbolic of all that was in opposition to Israel and to faith. This Warrior is seen approaching, not wounded nor weary, but glorious in apparel, and full of strength; and the prophet inquires, " Who is this? "

The answer to the inquiry comes from the Warrior Himself, " I that speak in righteousness, mighty to save." The words are brief, but they gather up into themselves all the values of the teaching of the recent parts of

the book. They are the words of Jehovah,
and they declare both His method and His
purpose. His method is that of speaking in
righteousness; His purpose is that of salvation, for the accomplishment of which He is
mighty.

2. *The Conflict*

Recognizing the person of the Warrior, the
prophet immediately inquires why His apparel
is red, and His garments like one " that tread-
eth in the wine-fat." The vision is that of
One Whose garments are sprinkled with blood
in evidence of a conflict, from which He is
emerging in victory. Of this appearance the
prophet demands an explanation.

The answer is immediately given, and it
first affirms the fact that alone, and without help from the peoples, the Warrior
has, in anger and in fury, overcome all His
foes.

The reason for His conflict is then declared
in the words, " For the day of vengeance was
in Mine heart, the year of My redeemed is
come." The acceptable year of the Lord has
passed, and the day of vengeance is also now
accomplished. The Warrior has overcome in
the strength of His wrath; but the passion

of that strength has been that of the redemption of His own.

Again the story of His loneliness in conflict is told. There was none to help, but His own strength was sufficient; and all the foes opposing Him, His purpose, and His people, are overcome and destroyed.

An interpretation of this passage which suggests that it describes in any sense the work of Christ at His first advent, must result in the most hopeless confusion. This is not a picture of the wounding of the Servant of God, but of the wounding and destruction of all His foes. The actual field of blood is not seen, but only the Conqueror, as having at last, in vengeance and in fury, swept away the enemies of His people and His purpose, He returns in victory, and the year of His redeemed begins.

b. THE PRAYER OF DESIRE

This whole prayer would seem to be of the nature of an interpolation upon the main teaching of this final section, which is resumed when the prophecy deals with the operation of discrimination in the sifting of the people.

The vision of the Warrior and His declarations appealed to the prophet. He was sensible of the absolute justice of the judgment described, and recognized that only by such activity could there be any hope. He therefore broke out into praise and prayer.

1. *Praise and Confession*

In language full of beauty the prophecy first describes the faithfulness of Jehovah to His people in the past. It declares the determination to make mention of the lovingkindnesses of Jehovah, of His goodness toward the house of Israel; and then gives two illustrations, the first of which describes His compassion for them in Egypt from which He was their Saviour; and the second, all His tender care of them during the period of their wilderness experiences. Thus His description looks back to the days in which, in spite of their rebellion and their grieving of His Holy Spirit, He cared for them and carried them.

This produces confession of the fact that by rebellion and grieving of the Spirit He was necessarily "turned to be their enemy."

All this does but serve to renew the song of His loving-kindnesses, and the prophecy celebrates His remembrance of His people, His remembrance of how they had been delivered from Egypt, and of that consequent new deliverance wherein He brought them to rest, out of the wilderness into the land.

2. *The Prayer*

The praise and confession merge into a prayer, which is the prayer of one profoundly conscious of failure and of desolation; but equally conscious of the goodness and grace of the heart of Jehovah. It is first an expression of need, and then a cry of anguish. This is followed by remembrance of past Divine activity and confession of sin. Finally it is the cry to Jehovah to act on behalf of His people.

α. The sore Need

In immediate and striking contrast with that rest which Jehovah gave to His people long ago, the prophecy describes the present condition as it appeals to Jehovah to observe it. The people are without evidences of the presence of God; without His power, as is suggested by the inquiry, " Where is Thy zeal and Thy mighty acts? "; and without His pity, as is suggested by the declaration, " The yearning of Thy bowels and Thy compassions are restrained toward me." That is the picture of the need, and the prayer utters its supreme argument as it declares, " Thou art our Father. . . . Thou art our Father; our Redeemer." That need makes its own urgent appeal to Jehovah to return. The rest was soon broken, the people possessed but a little while, and the sanctuary of God is broken down, while the people themselves have become as those over whom Jehovah has never had rule.

β. *The Cry*

This statement of need is followed by a great cry of anguish in the form of an appeal to Jehovah to rend the heavens, and to come in judgment against the adversaries. The cry is evidently the outcome of the vision of the Warrior, and expresses the earnest longing for the fulfilment of the process of judgment.

γ. *The Remembrance*

The great prayer changes its tone as looking back again to previous deliverances it remembers how Jehovah had in time past done exactly what now was sought. The mountains had flowed down from His presence. The principle is remembered that God works for him that waiteth for Him; that He meets with him that rejoiceth and worketh righteousness.

δ. *The Confession*

This remembrance produces a new confession of sin, and of the judgment which has fallen upon sin, as its necessary and proper result. God had been wroth, but the reason was that the people had sinned. They had continued long in the sin, and the question, " Shall we be saved? " expresses the profoundest sense of the sin. Uncleanness and pollution result in fading and in destruction. The final word of confession is that " there is none that calleth upon Thy name." It is an admission of the truth spoken by the Warrior, that when He looked, there was none to help.

ε. *The Cry*

The confession being made, the prayer ends in a great appeal. This appeal, opening with

the word "But," is in all likelihood based
upon that declaration of the Warrior to which
we have made reference. He saw there was
none to help, but He brought salvation. The
confession has admitted that there is none that
calleth upon the name of Jehovah. Nevertheless the cry is raised for deliverance.

The first note of it is that of submission.
It recognizes that God is Father, that He is
the potter. All the ruin of the people has
resulted from their rebellion against these
fundamental truths. That submission is made
the basis of an appeal that Jehovah will not
remember iniquity for ever, because the people
are His. The final argument of the cry is the
condition of the city of God. It is a wilderness, a desolation. The sanctuary is burned
with fire, and all the pleasant things are laid
waste.

c. THE SIFTING OF THE PEOPLE

The first impression made by the opening words of this section is that it constitutes an answer to the prayer of desire. A closer examination will almost certainly lead to the conclusion that this is not so. The prayer which we have considered is one characterized by absolute sincerity, and is that of the prophet, or of the remnant of whom he is the spokesman. Our present section contains words that cannot describe such a person or people.

Treating the prayer as we suggested, as being an interpolation upon the main teaching, we find that now the Warrior seen in the first vision, again takes up His manifesto. Being victorious over His foes, and those of His chosen people, He now proceeds to deal with His own. In this section therefore we have a graphic description of the working of the principle of discrimination in the sifting of the people by God. The distinction is first drawn between the false and the true; the result of the sifting is then described; and finally the new order resulting is revealed.

1. *The False and the True*

The Divine distinction between the false and the true, even among His own people, is very clearly marked in this section, as it first describes the rebellious; then recognizes the remnant; and finally utters the doom of the rebellious.

α. *The Rebellious*

The opening words, " I am inquired of by them that asked not for Me; I am found of them that sought Me not: I said, Behold Me, behold Me, unto a nation that was not called by My name," have no reference to Israel. Paul in his Roman letter cites them in such a way as to make this evident.[1] Thus it becomes all the more evident that this is a continuation of the manifesto of the Warrior. As the result of His judgment of the nations, He has brought them to recognition of Himself.

In striking contrast to this the rebellious among His people are described. His attitude toward them has been that of long-continued patience; " I have spread out My hands all the day," to which attitude they have replied by persistent rebellion, walking in a way that

[1] See " Analyzed Bible. Epistle to Romans," page 153.

is not good, after their own thoughts; which
description recalls the great appeal made by
the prophet subsequently to the description
of the work of the suffering Servant of God,
where the ways and thoughts of the people
are contrasted with the ways and thoughts of
God.

Moreover, this rebellion has expressed itself
in the most terrible practices of idolatry, and
all the abominations connected therewith.
The final fact in their sin was that of the
hypocrisy which assumed the attitude of su-
periority over other peoples, in that they had
said, " Stand by thyself, come not near to
me, for I am holier than thou."

These people were an offence to Jehovah
and His determination to visit them with
punishment is distinctly described.

β. The Seed

The judgment is to be discriminative, because of the remnant, who in spite of prevailing failure, are loyal to Jehovah. This is
taught by the figure of the wine found in the
clusters. The activity of discrimination is to
be that of bringing forth a seed out of Jacob,
and out of Judah an inheritor; and the issue
of discrimination is poetically described in the

words, " Sharon shall be a fold of flocks, and
the valley of Achor a place for herds to lie
down in, for My people that have sought Me."

γ. The Doom of the Rebellious

The message immediately returns to a yet
more definite and detailed declaration of the
doom that must fall upon the rebellious. Their
sin consists in their forsaking of Jehovah, and
forgetfulness of His holy mountain, and their
turning to idolatries.

These are destined to the sword, and must
bow down to slaughter; and again the reason
is declared that when Jehovah called, they did
not answer; when He spake, they did not hear,
but continued in evil courses.

2. The Result of the Sifting

The result of this process of sifting is then
graphically described. The experience of the
servants of Jehovah is contrasted with that of
the rebellious people. The former are brought
into the place of fulness and satisfaction.
They eat, they drink, they rejoice, they sing.
The latter are brought into the place of empti-
ness and sorrow. They are hungry, they are
thirsty, they are ashamed, they cry and howl.

Finally the destiny of the rebellious and the good is placed in contrast. The rebellious leave their name for a curse, and are slain. The servants of Jehovah receive a new name; and by the fulfilment of the principle of relationship to the God of truth, find the secret of continuity.

3. *The New Order*

The ultimate issue of this process of sifting is the setting up of the new order, the establishment of the kingdom of God.

This is first described in the terms of the creation, a new heavens and a new earth created, in which there shall be no remembrance of the former things.

At the centre of that new order so far as the earth is concerned, there will be the new city of God, Jerusalem, a rejoicing, inhabited by a people who are described as a joy; such a city and people as give joy to God, because weeping and crying are no more heard.

The life of the people under these new conditions will stand in vivid contrast to all the conditions of desolation which have lasted so long. Life itself will be of prolonged duration. Life will no longer be cut off in infancy, nor become prematurely old. To die at the

age of a hundred years will be considered
premature, the death of a child; and a mark-
ing of the displeasure of God against sin.

The conditions of toil will be altered entirely
in that the profits, that is, the values and results will belong to the toilers. Men will
build houses and inhabit them; they will plant
and eat. No words are needed to emphasize
the contrast between these conditions, and
those obtaining even at the present hour in
human history.

Moreover, the life of the people will be a life
of fellowship with God, a life of prayer heard
and answered.

The final note of description is one which
emphasizes the triumph of peace; the restoration of Nature to harmony, and the elimina-
tion of all ferocity, and the forces of destruction.

Thus end the great prophecies of peace.
They have proceeded through a declaration of
purpose, a description of the Prince, and teaching concerning the programme.

A comparison of the closing message of the
first book containing the prophecies of judgment with this final word of the prophecies of
peace will show the remarkable identity of
thought.

There the prophet declared, " Behold, your

God will come with vengeance, with the recompense of God; He will come and save you"; and this affirmation is followed by a description which ends with the words, "No lion shall be there, nor shall any ravenous beast go up thereon, they shall not be found there; but the redeemed shall walk there: and the ransomed of the Lord shall return, and come with singing to Zion; and everlasting joy shall be upon their heads: they shall obtain gladness and joy, and sorrow and sighing shall flee away."

The final paragraph of the prophecies of peace, following a description of the day of vengeance of God, opens, "Behold, I create new heavens and a new earth," and closes, "They shall not hurt nor destroy in all My holy mountain, saith the Lord."

EPILOGUE

This final section is of the nature of an epilogue. The second prophetic division of the book opened with a prologue in which the burden of its messages was declared to be that of comfort for afflicted Jerusalem. Its principal divisions have been separated by the declarations; "There is no peace, saith Jehovah, unto the wicked"; "There is no peace, saith my God, to the wicked." The thought of these declarations is repeated and elaborated in this final message. The whole teaching of the division is a revelation of Jehovah's determination to establish peace; but the fact that peace can never be established save upon the foundation of purity is never lost sight of. At last the prophet, with all the facts before him, of surrounding desolation and abounding sin, and of the established throne and persistent government of Jehovah, utters his final message. It falls into three parts; the last message to the formalists; the last message to the remnant; the last message to the world.

a. THE LAST MESSAGE TO THE FORMALISTS

The last word to the formalists consists of a declaration concerning true worship; a de-

nunciation of false worship; and the announcement of judgment thereupon.

1. *True Worship*

In the declaration concerning true worship
the prophecy reaches one of the most exalted
positions of Old Testament writing. The
prophet first declared heaven to be the throne,
and earth the footstool of Jehovah; and by
questions, revealed the truth that no place
of worship created by man can either contain
or confine Jehovah. All the things of which
men would construct a temple have first been
made by Jehovah. Therefore the inference is
that the whole earth is sacred, and any place
may be a place of worship.

This is further emphasized as he revealed
the true spirit of worship, and declared that
Jehovah receives the man who is of a poor
and contrite spirit, and trembles at His word.

2. *False Worship*

This declaration of what true worship is,
prepares the way for his fierce denunciation
of false worship. The expression of false
worship is described by four things which in
themselves are true and ordained in the econ-

omy of the chosen people; the killing of an ox, the sacrificing of a lamb, the offering of an oblation, and the burning of frankincense; but which things partake of the nature of four of the hateful practices of idolatry, the slaying of a man, the breaking of a dog's neck, the offering of swine's blood, and the blessing of an idol.

Thus false worship means the vitiation of true things, and the prophet proceeded to declare how this vitiation takes place. It is the result of disloyalty of heart. The people who choose their own ways, and delight in their abominations, degrade the true ceremonies of religion. Such ceremonies thus degraded are as hateful to God as are the abominations of idolatry.

3. *Judgment*

The judgment of formalism is then declared. Its form is to be that of delusions and fears, which Jehovah will Himself bring upon them.

The prophet was again careful to declare the reason of the judgment to be the indifference of the people to Jehovah, and their persistence in wickedness.

b. THE LAST MESSAGE TO THE REMNANT

The prophet immediately turned from the formalists to that remnant of faithful souls, who amid all the desolations have been true to Jehovah.

1. *The Word of Comfort*

They are described as obedient, in that they tremble at His word; as persecuted, in that they are hated of their brethren, and cast out for the sake of the name. The word of comfort to them is that not they, but the people who have persecuted them, shall be ashamed.

2. *The Travail of Jerusalem*

Then in forceful and graphic language he described the travail of Jerusalem. There is a voice of tumult from the city, a voice from the temple. It is the voice of Jehovah Who renders recompense to His enemies. All this means the travail and pain of the city, but the result of it is cited in language true to the figure. There is the birth of a man child. It is a thing of wonder that a land shall be born in a day, and a nation be brought forth at once; but it is nevertheless a fact, because Jehovah has brought to the birth, and consequently the travail of Jerusalem is her way into triumph.

3. *The Triumph of Jerusalem*

This leads him immediately to a description of the triumph of Jerusalem. The remnant are called upon to rejoice with her, and be glad for her, because of her restoration. Her children are to be satisfied within her, because Jehovah will extend peace to her like a river.

The final word of comfort is one of the most tender and beautiful in the whole of the Scriptures. "As one whom his mother comforteth, so will I comfort you; and ye shall be comforted in Jerusalem." It is an unveiling of the tenderest fact in the nature of God, and the result of it will be that the faithful souls who have been persecuted, and have suffered, will rejoice and flourish in the more perfect knowledge of Jehovah.

c. THE LAST MESSAGE TO THE WORLD

The final movement in the epilogue is one characterized by breadth of outlook, and generality of statement. In it the prophet repeated in language full of dignity, his declaration of the coming of God as fire to judgment; declaring the wider issues to follow in the history of the world; and finally announcing the destiny of good and evil.

1. *The Coming in Fire*

The description of the coming of Jehovah in fire emphasizes its majesty. His chariots will be like the whirlwind in order to render His anger with fury, and His rebuke with flames of fire. The coming will be one of might as He pleads with all flesh, and searches out and destroys the evil, gathering all nations and tongues to the manifestation of His glory.

2. *The Wider Issues*

This leads to the declaration of the wider issues. The sign is to be set, and the news is to be spread to all the nations and to the isles afar off, that have never heard of His fame, with the result that all exiles, however far scattered, will be brought to Jerusalem as an offering to Jehovah.

3. *The Destiny*

The ultimate word is one full of august solemnity as it describes the irrevocable destiny of good and of evil. The new heavens and the new earth which Jehovah creates will remain before Him, as will also the people who fear His name; and the passing of the seasons will witness the regular assembly of all flesh for the purpose of worshipping in His presence.

Those who have transgressed against Him are beyond hope, and their carcases abide in the perpetual corruption of the worm that dieth not, and the fire that is not quenched.

Thus the last word of the great prophecy; which has been uttered under the inspiration of the vision of the unshaken throne of Jehovah, a prophecy the burden of which is that of the Divine purpose of peace, and which first describes how judgment proceeds to peace, and secondly describes the peace which issues from judgment; is a note of solemn warning, which may be expressed in the words already twice repeated, " There is no peace, saith my God, to the wicked."